The Media on *This is True* . . .  S0-AZP-019

"For years, Cassingham has been searching the papers for amazing but true stories or headlines, to which he attaches a witty, funny, or borderline-sarcastic tagline. It's nearly impossible to read these and not laugh out loud."

Philadelphia Daily News

"Randy Cassingham has a passion for the truth. And you'll never believe the stuff he's dug up.... Truly stranger than fiction."

USA Today

"With so many rumours doing the rounds on the Net, it's often hard to sort the fact from the fiction. Randy Cassingham has made it his mission in life to bring unusual stories to the attention of a Net-using audience."

London Daily Telegraph

"This is True [has] one of the biggest [distribution] lists on the Net.... It's [*sic*] popularity comes from Cassingham's shrewd selection of subject matter."

Wired

"*This is True* came into being in 1994 when Cassingham... began clipping funny and bizarre items from newspapers, adding editorial comments to them and then posting them on the employee bulletin board at NASA's Jet Propulsion Laboratory in Pasadena, Calif., where he worked. It became an intra-office hit."

Rocky Mountain News

"Randy skims about 500 newspaper articles per day, and distills from them summaries of the strangest news stories — the ones that make you turn your head and say, 'They did *what?*'"

Contentious

"The column consists of ... recent news stories that comes with his droll remarks added in just a few words. God, these stories are so interesting that really, they need no decoration entirely!"

Chinabyte (translated from Chinese)

What *True*'s Readers Say . . . .

"You do a wonderful job of finding and passing on unusual stories. I sit and read some of these stories with my mouth agape, some of them I read with my eyes wide and eyebrows up in surprise, some of them make me laugh, and some of them make me roll my eyes and smirk. Keep up the *great* work!!"

Suz, North Carolina

"*True* provides a wonderful source of material when preparing sermons for Sunday services! The real life angle, and the humorous punchlines, always work well as illustrations."

Pastor Rus, New York

"Great work! My father told me to mention that your humorous lines at the end of the news stories remind him very much of Bob Hope's incredible one-liners."

Adam, California

"After stealing a few minutes here and there from my children, I have finally managed to finish all three books my sister sent me from New York. Now, I'm all sad. I don't have any more of your books to read. Obviously, you will let us know when the next book comes out?"

Natacha, United Kingdom

"The world is a strange place, and you seem to know about most of it. Thanks for all the *news*.

Monte, Washington DC

"Wicked, man. Great stuff. Thank you for the irreverence and wit."

Augusto, Brazil

"I just wanted to say thanks for helping make the beginning of my day a very special one. I'm recovering from breast cancer and laughing is one of the best healers I can think of to help get through. Please keep up the wonderful work you're doing. Much love & many hugs."

Patti, New York

This is True®:
Artificial Intelligence Like Real Thing
And 500 Other Bizarre-but-True Stories and Headlines From the World's Press

The *This is True* Collection, Volume Four

This is True®:
Artificial Intelligence Like Real Thing
And 500 Other Bizarre-but-True Stories
and Headlines From the World's Press

The *This is True* Collection, Volume Four

---

by

Randy Cassingham

Freelance Communications
Boulder, Colorado

Published by Freelance Communications
Post Office Box 17326
Boulder, Colorado, 80308 USA

9 8 7 6 5 4 3 2 1

Printed and bound in the United States of America using non-pe-
troleum ink on acid-free paper.

International Standard Book Number: 0-935309-24-1

Preface . . . .

Welcome to the the fourth *This is True* collection. *True* is a weekly collection of bizarre-but-true news stories with running commentary, plus an actual "headline of the week", that is sold to newspapers and magazines as a feature column. (The first three volumes of the collection, *This is True: Deputy Kills Man With Hammer*, *This is True: Glow-in-Dark Plants Could Help Farmers*, and *This is True: Pit Bulls Love You, Really,* are also available — see your bookseller, or the last page of this book, to order. The titles come from real newspaper headlines.)

I like to make it clear what is it I mean by "true". *True*'s stories don't come from the tabloids or underground newspapers, but rather from the legitimate/mainstream print media, such as national and international news wires, city newspapers, and major newsweeklies like *Newsweek.* But let me caution you: take everything you read in newspapers — and even in *This is True* — with at least a small grain of salt. In addition to my job as a writer, I've worked a few other careers, including a brief stint as a sheriff deputy, several years as a paramedic, and ten years at a NASA field center. One thing in common in all of these jobs is that I have often been a participant in, or direct observer of, events that tend to end up on the news or in the paper. And not once, when I knew the entire story, did any news report on the event come without at least some small error in the "facts".

So I watch carefully for corrections. Whenever I've discovered that an item in *This is True* was based on a "fact" taken in error, or indeed if I've made an error myself, the item has been corrected. But I have resisted the temptation to improve (beyond grammar or typos) my comments — they are as they were written under deadline pressure.

In addition to the print outlets that carry *This is True,* readers can subscribe and get it on the Internet. For details on that, please see <http://www.thisistrue.com>. You'll be happy to note that even if you've read *True* every week in the newspaper — or online — you still have not read every story in this book. I very often have leftover stories which don't fit in the weekly column (newspapers enforce a word limit). Some weeks have them, some don't, but there are quite a few stories mixed in throughout, plus a section of leftover headlines at the end. Fortunately for me, there is never a shortage of material about the weird things we humans do.

The stories for *This is True* come from "legitimate" printed news media, both American and international. I try as much as possible to credit the original source. For example, if a story is taken from a newspaper, but the newspaper credits a wire service as the source, I do too — I don't necessarily credit the paper I found the story in. Thus the most-cited sources in this book are the major news wires:

- AP (Associated Press)
- Reuters* (Reuters Ltd.)
- AFP (Agence France-Presse)
- UPI (United Press International)

This volume compiles columns released to syndication from June, 1997 through the end of July, 1998.

I enjoy hearing from readers. My e-mail address is included on my web site. After you've had a chance to peruse the stories and headlines here, drop me a line and let me know what you think.

Randy Cassingham
Boulder, Colorado

Edited by Cathie Walker
Book and Cover Design by Freelance Communications

---

*   For years, Reuters slugged their stories "Reuter", so I did too. In 1997, they changed their attribution tag to "Reuters", so the text in this book reflects this new usage.

This is True:
Artificial Intelligence Like Real Thing

Taste of Victory: The Hollywood Wax Museum in southern California has moved its statue of boxer Mike Tyson from its Sports Hall of Fame. Owner Raubi Sundher said that after seeing Tyson cheat in his fight against Evander Holyfield and "chewing the idea over," he moved the statue to the Chamber of Horrors next to Hannibal "the Cannibal" Lecter. (UPI) ...*Tyson doesn't even deserve that honor — he's just a two-bit boxer.*

Ski Don't: Ricardo Enamorado, 30, has been rescued. The man had gone for a ride on a water scooter on Lake Michigan, but it stalled. He was found two days later, just 500 yards off the Chicago shore. "He was just sitting there, waiting on us to get to him," a Coast Guard spokesman said. A hospital spokeswoman said Enamorado was in good condition, suffering from sunburn and dehydration. It was unclear why Enamorado did not swim to shore, nor why he spent two days in the water without drinking any — Lake Michigan is a freshwater lake. (AP) ...*Water, water everywhere, but not a drop of think.*

Sex Ed: Officials at Jacobus College in Enschede, Netherlands, have expelled a 17-year-old student for running a prostitution ring from school. It wasn't the nature of his business that bothered the administrators, it was his booking appointments during class on a cellular telephone that did it. "What he does in his free time is his own business," a teacher insisted. "But we did try to make it clear that it couldn't be tolerated during school time." The boy was getting good grades. (Reuters) ... *"Study to be quiet, and to do your own business." —1 Thessalonians 4:11.*

Twelve Shows, Rerun Constantly: Bill Moses expects people to make jokes about his new TV channel, the Recovery Network. "If people can make fun of us, that's a good thing," he insists. The cable channel is for alcoholics and other substance abusers who don't want to go to meetings, such as those put on by Alcoholics Anonymous. "By delivery into the privacy of one's home, you get rid of a lot of the stigma and hesitation" of seeking help, Moses says. Moses is quick to add that the channel will be "sensitively selective" about the advertising it accepts. No beer commercials. (AP) ...*Sure hope there will be a lengthy series dealing with television addiction.*

Would You Like Fries With That? Anti-abortion activists are outraged that a London clinic plans to offer quick service, "lunch hour" abortions at several of its facilities. "They have a right to the best service possible," says the director of Marie Stopes International, a British charity named for a birth control advocate. Critics say the three- to four-minute procedure trivializes abortion. "This would be the ultimate in a fast economy, you have fast food and now you can have a fast abortion," said one. (Reuters) ...*It was probably conceived in a hurry, too.*

Be Prepared: Rita Rupp of Tulsa, Okla., was scared about driving cross-country, but she and her husband Floyd needed to get to New York for a wedding. Just to be safe, she pre-wrote a note that she could leave for someone to find in case of trouble. "Help Kidnaped Call Highway Patrol," the note read. "My Ford Van Cream & Blue Oklahoma." It also listed her name and telephone number. All went well until Rita and Floyd got to Auburn, Mass., where Mrs. Rupp accidentally dropped the note during a bathroom break. Police issued an all points bulletin, but didn't spot the van. The case received news media attention for 24 hours until Floyd called his office to check for messages. "He said, 'I'm sitting here enjoying the view of the ocean'," Rupp's office manager told reporters after the call. "You have no idea what's going on, do you?" the manager replied. (AP) ...*Sounds like that might be a common state of affairs for the Rupps.*

Sir-plus: An auction of 26 manorial titles in London netted nearly 400,000 pounds (US$663,000). "I inherited them, but they haven't any particular significance for me," an unidentified lord at the sale said, noting he had several to spare. Another seller noted such sales aren't new. "These things have always been bought and sold, dating back as far as William the Conqueror and the Doomsday Book in 1086." The new Lord of Chuderleigh thinks his title, purchased for a bargain 7,500 pounds, could have a practical benefit. "It might well help us to get a dinner reservation somewhere," he said. (Reuters) ...*Typical: just hungry for power.*

Priorities Straight: Politicians in Green Bay, Wis., are steamed that the community would not allow any politicians in its Fourth of July parade. "They allow horses, donkeys and clowns, but they won't allow us," fumed state Rep. John Ryba. "We're not good enough." (AP) ...*Correct. Did you have some sort of point?*

A Fool and His Money are Soon Parted: Even after paying his lawyers, Rodney King still has some of the $3.8 million left from his civil judgement against the city of Los Angeles for the 1991 beating he got by city police officers. "We want to give a real positive boost to the rap market," King said of his new venture, Straight Alta-Pazz Recording Co. The company has recorded an album for the group Stranded, "California Grindin", and is now looking for a distributor. (AP) ...*First I was beat up / now I'll sing this song / Just to ask the burnin' question / can't we all just get along?*

At Least, as Long as You're Clear We're Talking About Popular Music, and Not Certificates of Deposit

Gen Xers Love Parents
More than CDs

UPI headline

Look Out Below: Eric Barcia, 22, had always heard about "bungee jumping" and wanted to try it. Not having the specialized elastic cords experienced jumpers use, he collected a number of bungee tie-down cords, the kind with hooks on the ends, and connected them together with electrical tape at each joint to make sure the hooks wouldn't come undone. He brought his home-made lifeline to a railroad trestle in Springfield, Va., tied it off, and jumped. Police were called to investigate when Barcia was killed after hitting the ground at full speed. "The length of the cord that he had assembled was greater than the distance between the trestle and the ground," a police spokesman said. Barcia's grandmother couldn't understand why he screwed up so badly. "He was very smart in school," she remembered. (AP) *...If that's how you want to interpret the teacher's comment that he was "about as sharp as a bowling ball," then fine.*

Be All That You Can Be: Earl Christensen, 18, a Montrose, Colo., high school student, was assigned to write an essay about "why government doesn't work". He wrote it as a letter, which he mailed to State Sen. Ben Alexander, chairman of the Senate Education Committee. In his letter, "I said I didn't like the way the military was presented to youth," Christensen told reporters. "I said I thought it's not the war on drugs, but it's war on the American public that choose to use drugs." Alexander was so upset with the student's critique that he asked Christensen to meet with him. At the meeting, Alexander lectured, "A lot of people fought and died so you could stay here and waste your life on drugs," and added that Christensen was a "worthless piece of shit." Christensen walked out, and won't take Alexander's calls of apology. (Denver Post) *...Sounds like Alexander is a few troops short of a battalion.*

School Assignments II: Parents in Riverside, Calif., are upset with a Norte Vista High School math teacher who asked some unusual questions on a summer school test, such as "[A man] is in prison sentenced to six years for murder. He got $10,000 for the hit. If his common-law wife is spending $100 per month, how much money will be left when he gets out of prison and how many years will he get after he kills her for spending the money?" The teacher said the test was a joke, has apologized to the students and "is more than willing to apologize to anybody who is offended," the teacher's union says. But Louise Palomarez of the Mexican Political Association says "We want him fired! We don't want no damn apology." (AP) *...Señora! Write "We don't want any damned apology" on the board 50 times.*

Read the Label: Two unlicenced exterminators in Biloxi, Miss., Paul Walls, 62, and Dock Eatman, 64, were sentenced to serve federal prison terms of 78 months and 63 months, respectively, after they used an agricultural pesticide to treat hundreds of houses. The pesticide, which is safe to use on cotton crops since the sun breaks it down, is fatal to humans in doses as small as a teaspoon. The houses had to be destroyed. "I did not know that this stuff was like they said it was," Eatman claimed. "I got it in my own mouth and my eyes and I washed it out with olive oil and it never hurt or killed me." (Reuters) ...*More's the pity.*

Where Do You Want to Go Today? Police in Issaquah, Wash., surrounded a townhouse building after one of the residents reported shots fired in one of the units. They eventually coaxed an unnamed 43-year-old man out, and discovered the problem. He was so frustrated with his computer that he shot it to death. The cabinet had four bullet holes, the monitor one. A file cabinet also took a slug, as did a wall. "We don't know if it wouldn't boot up or what," a police spokesman said. No one was injured. The man was taken away for a mental evaluation. (AP) ... *"Another 'fatal exception 0E in kernel32.exe'? I'll show you a what a **real** fatal exception is!"*

I've Got The Blues: Stories of the listings of toll-free "hot lines" with typos, resulting in callers getting a "phone sex" service, are so numerous as to not even be unusual anymore. But two recent cases stand out from the crowd. The number for the U.S. Equal Employment Opportunity Commission in Chicago, where one would call to report sexual harassment, turned out to have such a typo in Ameritech's Chicago directory. It's listed in the directory's "Blue Pages", and the error was not discovered for six months. Then there's the phone sex company who got a new toll-free number — after a suicide hot line in Columbia, S.C., dropped it. The phone company accidentally left the listing in the Columbia phone book. "This is not the kind of message a suicidal person needs to hear," said a spokeswoman for the Alliance for the Mentally Ill in South Carolina. The father of a boy who had recently attempted suicide complained, "How many... kids have called and got that kind of stuff and just said, 'Well, I give up'?" (UPI, AP) ...*More likely it made them realize they had a reason to live after all.*

Roughing It: Chris Wearstler, 21, had gone out for a four-day hike in Washington's Olympic National Park, but got lost when he went looking for water. After nine days, long out of food and water, he heard flutes and bagpipes and walked toward them. "I thought there was a music festival in the woods," he said later. "I was on my way to the festival." There was no music, but he managed to walk into the arms of rescuers out looking for him. "He was apparently beginning to hallucinate," park ranger Curt Sauer said. Wearstler said other than getting lost, he enjoyed his trip. "If I would have had food, it would have been a really cool experience," he said. (AP) ...*Kind of like everyday life in the Third World.*

Easy Come, Easy Go: When Miss Canada International Danielle House was convicted of assault after a barroom brawl, pageant officials stripped her of her title. "Yes she has lost her title," a spokeswoman confirmed. "Because she is a role model, we cannot condone someone convicted of assault." (Reuters) ...*Forget the jeweled crown; award her the golden gloves!*

Long Jump: Two British motorcyclists "roaring" through Amsterdam drove at high speed into what they thought was a tunnel. It was, instead, the entrance to an underground parking garage. They hit a concrete barrier and "were more or less launched from their mounts and landed about 10 meters further on," a police spokesman said. The bikes were destroyed; the men suffered moderate injuries. (Reuters) ...*Thus failing their High Performance Parking class.*

U.F.O.
Russian, U.S. Astronauts from Different Worlds
Reuters headline

We Bend Over Backwards to be Friendly: Mugs Away Saloon in San Clemente, Calif., recently celebrated its annual mooning day. That's when bar patrons drop their pants and crack a smile at passing Amtrak trains. More than 20 customers "of all sexes and ages" participated. When asked why, one man responded, "Where else can you do this and get away with it?" (AP) ...*Prison.*

Busted: Bennie Casson is suing. He was in P.T.'s Show Club in Sauget, Ill., where he claims that dancer Busty Heart hit him with her 88-inch breasts, which reportedly weigh 40 pounds each. Casson's suit says he suffered "emotional distress, mental anguish and indignity," as well as his neck, shoulder and back being "bruised, contused, lacerated and made sore" by Heart's "slamming her breasts into his neck and head region, all without legal justification, provocation or consent." He's asking for $200,000 in damages. (Knight-Ridder) ...*He'll need at least that much for his divorce settlement.*

Overaccessorized: Bettie Phillips, 54, of Hiddenite, N.C., "adopted" a two-month-old fawn she says she found on the side of a road. Police were tipped off that the deer's ears had been pierced, and it was wearing earrings. The fawn was turned over to a wildlife center, which treated its ears for infection. Phillips has been charged with animal cruelty for the piercings, for which she didn't volunteer an explanation, and with illegally possessing wildlife. (AP) ...*Remember: to legally pierce a deer, you need a license and you must do it from a sporting distance.*

Yard Sale: When Sam Kaplan, 65, was seen standing by a road in Tampa, Fla., holding a sign that read, "Want Wife", the story was covered in local newspapers. He told reporters he was a retired millionaire who wanted to settle down, and was contacted by "several" eligible women who saw the story. But someone who knew Kaplan sent a copy of the article to Kaplan's wife. She was not amused. Linda Kaplan said her husband walked out on her two and a half years ago "without even taking a toothbrush." When confronted by reporters, Kaplan admitted he was indeed still married. (UPI) ...*Be careful what you wish for — you might get it.*

Oh No, Pinocchio: Italians admit they are chronic liars. Riza Psicosomatica, an Italian psychology magazine, reports that 70 percent of Italians surveyed admit to telling five to ten lies every day. "Don't worry about it, it's all been taken care of," was the most commonly reported lie. Other well-worn fibs included "I'll always love you," "That looks great on you" and "How nice to

see you." (Reuters) ...*You can't trust those results — they may
have been lying to the pollsters.*

Always Use a Modem: Grandmotherly sex therapist Ruth Wes-
theimer was given a tour of computer giant Microsoft's headquarters. She is worried about the employees — Dr. Ruth says it's
difficult to "have time to have good sex if you work 80 hours a
week." And forget cybersex: she told employees that "Human
relationships and laughter and touching cannot be replaced by any
computer." (AP) ...*Somehow, "good sex," "micro" and "soft"
don't seem to be compatible concepts.*

Northern Exposure: Thanks to a court decision in Ontario, Canada, it is now legal for women there to go topless in public — at
least, anywhere a man can go without a shirt. But Heather Generaux, 38, didn't appreciate that equal rights concept when she
saw a neighbor, Jennifer Fitzgibbon, 23, sunning herself topless
in her Trenton back yard where Generaux's 10-year-old son could
see her. Generaux pleaded guilty to assault charges after a witness
said she climbed over a hedge, kicked Fitzgibbon in the stomach,
and "ripped her bikini bottom clear off her body." (UPI) ...*Apparently she didn't think her son could see well enough.*

Back to School: A student at Quincy (Mass.) High School arrested
17 students on drug charges. The student, actually a 32-year-old
deputy sheriff, spent seven months attending the school to root
out drug problems. Even the principal and teachers didn't know
his true identity. His grades were so good, especially for a
"troubled student", that he had to cut class to make them drop. He
explained his thinning hair and wrinkles by claiming he abused
steroids. "That guy sucks," complained one sophomore once the
truth was known. "You shouldn't do that to your friends. He acted
like he was friends." But another sophomore was more philo-
sophic: "The guy looked like he was 37 years old and everybody
knew," he said. "But I guess there were some people who were
stupid enough to believe it." (AP) ...*Isn't that one of the reasons
they call it dope?*

May I Make a Suggestion? After Dothan, Ala., Judge Lawson
Little sentenced Jerrick Michael Snell, 23, to prison for cocaine

possession, he happened to walk by the convict's courthouse cell. That's when Snell invited Little to ...*uh*... perform a sexual act on him. Little ordered that Snell be gagged and brought back to the courtroom, where he amended Snell's sentence. Instead of the 20 years in prison he got in court earlier, Snell has been sentenced to the maximum — life. (AP) ...*Where, likely, he'll have plenty of experience with the suggested sexual act.*

Men of the Cloth vs. Women with no Clothes: Strippers in Hurricane, W.Va., are astounded at some job offers they have received recently. From a local Baptist church. The jobs: plumbers, electricians or construction workers, and the offer includes free training. The church, led by Rev. Gerry White and located near the Lady Godiva's strip joint, raised $3,000 to lure the strippers away from their jobs. The strippers, however, don't think much of the offers. "I'm a dancer. I don't see anything wrong with being a dancer," says Amanda Rice, 21. "If I wanted another job, I could get another job." Another stripper agreed. "Where else am I going to make $280 a night and have so much fun?" asked Tiffany, who refused to give her real name. "Can you imagine me as a plumber?" (AP) ...*Strangely, yes: most people are used to seeing down what's inside plumbers' pants.*

Shop 'til You Drop: Barbara Morris was putting her groceries in her van in Louisville, Ky., when a man flashed a gun and ordered her to drive. "I said, 'Just take my car,' but it didn't work that way," she said. He forced her to go on a nine-hour shopping spree, buying $6,000 worth of laptop computers, fast food, VCRs, and cigarettes, all while covering her with his gun. If that wasn't weird enough, he also had her stop to make photocopies of the receipts so she could keep track of what was paid for with her checks and credit cards. "He was keeping the originals and giving me the copies," Morris said. "I just went along with whatever he said to do." A store manager finally got suspicious and called the police, who arrived in time to see her pushing a shopping cart full of cigarettes toward her van. The alleged gunman, Frederick Harris, 41, was changed with theft, kidnaping, robbery and gun violations. (AP) ...*Felony, or dream date? You be the judge.*

No Soup for You! Short-order cook Hashiem Zayed, 59, and waitress Helen Menicou, 47, had worked together for over 20 years at San Francisco's Pine Crest Diner. As she had apparently done many times in the past, she yelled at him in front of the customers, a police inspector says, telling him not to make poached eggs since the dish wasn't on the menu. "He says he just lost it," the inspector added. Zayed allegedly shot her once, chased her around the restaurant shooting her four more times, then asked the cashier to call the police while he waited outside to be taken into custody. He has been booked for murder. "He was having a bad day," the inspector explained. (AP) ...*Sounds like Helen's day kinda sucked too.*

Oh, Yeah, Like We're Really Going to Believe That

Poll: Americans Becoming More Cynical

UPI headline

Food Fight: An El Cerrito, Calif., woman has been charged with child abuse after her 13-year-old daughter ate herself to death. The child, whose calves were 47 inches around, weighed more than 680 pounds when she died. Mom said the girl had steadfastly refused to see a doctor for the last four years, and had not left their apartment for months. "She wouldn't cooperate," the mother explained. "When she has an appointment, what can I do? I can't pick her up and take her." (AP) ...*Not bringing the kid wheelbarrows full of food might have been a good start.*

Food Fight II: Despite the desire of the onlookers — and the sponsor — the home favorite for the Mustard Yellow International Belt was again bested by a Japanese contestant. The belt, the prize for the 82nd annual Nathan's Famous Hot Dog Eating Contest, goes to whoever can eat the most hot dogs, with buns, in 12 minutes. Hirofumi Nakajima, 135 pounds, ate 24 1/2 dogs. Ed "The Animal" Krachie, 330 pounds, the U.S.'s Great Wide Hope, pounded down a mere 20 weiners. In fact, he came in third, behind another Japanese man, 100-pound Kazutoyo "The Rabbit" Arai. "I don't know where they put it," Krachie said after the contest. "Both of those guys put together weigh less than me." Nakajima's secret: he alternated eating the dogs and the buns, rather than cramming both down together. (AP) ...*Perhaps next year, Krachie won't lose time by slathering on onions, mustard, kraut, chili, cheese, relish....*

Food Fight III: Mait Lepik is the winner of Estonia's first banana-eating contest. His secret: the rules said no assistants, so with no one to peel the bananas for him to save time, he ate them with the skins still on. Lepik managed to slip down 10 bananas in three minutes to capture the title. (AP) ...*Perhaps next year, Lepik will best that record by using Nakajima's secret, alternating eating the bananas and the skins, rather than cramming both down together.*

Yes, We Have No Bananas II: A Russian scientist has died in the worst atomic accident since the Chernobyl disaster. Alexander Zakharov emerged from a uranium-contaminated Arzamas-16 atomic weapons lab and told colleagues, "I told you, the gloves were too slippery." Zakharov absorbed more than 600 roentgen of radiation. A government commission investigating the accident didn't say how the slippery gloves contributed to the mishap, but confirmed "The gloves were like a banana skin that people slide on when they run too fast." (Reuters) ... *"But remember please, the Law by which we live / We are not built to comprehend a lie / We can neither love nor pity nor forgive. / If you make a slip in handling us you die." —Rudyard Kipling in "The Secret of the Machines".*

Yes No III: The former president of Zimbabwe has been charged with 11 counts of sodomy, attempted sodomy and indecent assault after an alleged homosexual relationship with an aide. Homosexuality and sodomy are illegal in Zimbabwe. The ex-president, a 61-year-old Methodist priest, is married and has four children. His name: Canaan Banana. (Reuters) ...*In the U.S., that would be known as a freak of nomenclature.*

Bottom Line: Michael Levitt, associate chief of staff at the Minneapolis Veterans Administration Hospital in Minnesota, says he thinks he has identified the ...*well*... offending component of flatulence: sulfur. "When we presented [volunteers with] samples with high concentrations of sulfur gas, people told us it didn't smell very good," Levitt said. "Then we removed sulfur gases chemically, and the odor disappeared." Phase II: they fitted test subjects with air-tight Mylar underpants, with a tube that routed any ...*um*... expelled gasses through a charcoal filter. Other volunteers then sniffed the output, and expressed their ...*uh*... approval of the underpants' effectiveness. Still, the filter isn't ideal. "Sulfur may come from the foods people eat, but we can't say just which foods people should avoid," Leavitt concluded. (UPI) ...*That's just like a government researcher: he attacked the problem at the wrong end.*

Pig in a Poke: It's an old, old joke. How do porcupines mate? Very, very carefully, the punch line goes. Researchers now report in the British journal New Scientist that indeed, that's how they do it. And the quills are sex attractants, they say. According to a five-year study, female porcupines are turned on by particularly large males who win fights with other males. "After a fight the loser can have anywhere between 30 to 50 quills stuck in his face and chest," one of the researchers said. "It must be extremely painful walking around with dozens of someone else's quills stuck in your face." (Reuters) ...*Not to mention how terribly difficult it must be to stay "safe" when using condoms.*

Clock Watcher: Although Malcolm Eccles, 50, died, his wife still has him around. At his suggestion ("Malcom was as daft as a brush," his widow says), the London, England, woman had a glass-blower make her an egg timer using Malcolm's cremated remains for the sand. He's kept in the kitchen. Now, he can "help me and it would be a nice way of remembering him," Brenda Eccles said. (Reuters) ...*In death just like in life: he lasts exactly three minutes.*

Profusely
Does TV Need To Apologize?
AP headline

I Wanna Be Famous: Now that Gianni Versace murder suspect Andrew Cunanan has killed himself, Modesto Cunanan has spoken out about his son. "He never saw violence in our household," the elder Cunanan said. "That was never part of his growing up years." However, he concedes it is possible his son did commit the several murders attributed to him during a cross-country spree. "I wouldn't discount the possibility that it did happen," Cunanan said. He added that his son's only stated ambition was, "I wanna be somebody." (AP) *...He should have been more specific.*

Birds of a Feather: "My wife, Kim, was telling Fred's wife, Wendy, about my owl watching and described how I got the birds to hoot back. She said: 'That's funny, that's just what Fred has been doing'," said Neil Simmons. Fred and Wendy are his neighbor in Stokeinteignhead, Devon, England. "Then the penny dropped. I felt such a twit when I found out." Fred and Neil had spent a year hooting to each other from their gardens every night, each thinking the other was a real owl. "I couldn't resist hooting at the owls. I was absolutely delighted when they hooted back," Fred Cornes said. "I never realized that I was fooling my neighbor who was fooling me." (UPI) *...There they go, hooting themselves in the foot again.*

Where the Boys Are: The Lowell (Mass.) School Committee was trying to figure out what to do about the troublemakers in local schools. "There are one, two or three students in each class who are full of mischief, who are disruptive," says committee member William Taupier. "It's a small number, around 2 percent, but the wrath they bring on the whole system is unfair to the other 98 percent." Then he got an idea: put them all in the same school together. "It's not going to be a case where you'll be exiled from school forever," Taupier said. "By a merit system they will return to the regular school system." (AP) *...Meanwhile, they'll have one hell of a football team.*

Knock Before Entering: Mustafa Khalil and Abdullah al-Amri have withdrawn a lawsuit against NASA after Yemen's Prosecutor General threatened to arrest them over their claim. The two sued the space agency for trespassing on Mars with the Pathfinder lander and Sojourner rover. "They said they received the planet as an inheritance from their ancestors and therefore rejected the landing of the U.S. spacecraft on Mars without their prior notification and permission," a Yemeni newspaper reported. "The two men are abnormal," prosecutor Mohammad al-Bady said. "By examining the case we found out they were only seeking fame and publicity." (Reuters) *...Arrest people that file stupid, publicity-seeking lawsuits? A capital idea, Mr. al-Bady.*

My Word is My Bond: "It was all done on the recommendation of the [District Attorney]," insists Levelland (Tex.) Municipal Judge Ron Wood. He had set the bail for rape suspect E.C. Stewart Jr. at "a zillion dollars". Stewart is accused of raping a woman twice, the second time while free on $10,000 bond after his arrest for the first attack. Wood said the zillion-dollar bail was to be sure Stewart stayed in jail and could not get to the woman again. "It was to simulate no bond," he added. (Lubbock Avalanche-Journal) *...Wasn't it "simulated justice" that led to his low bail the first time around?*

Having a Ball in South Florida, Wish You Were Here: A robber apparently didn't have a stocking to use as a mask when he hit a bank in Fort Myers Beach, Fla. His disguise: a beach ball with eye holes, and plastic bags over his hands. "I'm looking for a guy with a beach ball on his head," a Lee County sheriff's investigator said. "You don't see that every day." (AP) *...He needs to get out more: there are people with inflated heads all over the place.*

May it Please the Court: A New York state legal panel has ruled that Great Neck attorney Rosalie Osias has not violated any professional rules with her advertising, which features her in sexy clothing in an attempt to "crack the glass ceiling protecting the male-dominated corporate culture," she says. "I am delighted in what is clearly a total vindication of my position — even if it was prone," Osias purred. "Lawyers can now use plenty of cleavage and leg in advertising their law firms and their expertise." (UPI) *...Otherwise known as luring the moth to the flame.*

Playing with Matches: "We're going to get the drugs now," a 4-year-old boy says on a video tape turned over to McKean Township, Pa., police. The tape shows the mother paying a teen-aged pusher for some marijuana, then the lad saying "I want a hit! I want a hit! I want a hit!" The boy had difficulty lighting the pipe, but finally got it going and took a long drag as his mom watched from the background. The mother, Mary Jane Kline, 40, has been charged with corrupting a minor. The boy has been placed in foster care. (AP) *...Remember the good old days, when "mommy seen pushing son" referred to baby carriage outings in the park?*

Notice: Position is Still Open

Model Elle MacPherson
Denies Having 'Boy Toy'

Reuters headline

Pop Quiz: Faced with inquiries by 2,500 candidates for 35 openings for teachers, New York's Connetquot School District thought it should try to narrow the field to the best applicants. So it gave teacher wanna-be's an 11th grade English test. Nearly three-quarters failed the exam. (UPI) *...For the philosophy portion of the test, take a position for or against literacy in educators. Justify your position with examples, using at least one word with four syllables.*

No, It Wasn't in Bill's Handwriting: Can't understand the new 2,256-page tax bill signed by President Clinton? You won't be helped by errors which are inevitably included in the text, insiders say. Former director of the Congressional Budget Office Robert Reischauer says "There is always a technical-corrections bill" following complicated tax legislation. Such laws are often written in a rush or late at night by overworked staffers. Tax legislation passed by Congress in 1981 included a note scrawled in the margin on one page: "Call Rita" — complete with her telephone number. (Knight-Ridder) ... *"If you like laws and sausages, you should never watch either one being made." —Otto von Bismarck (1815–1898).*

First Wives Club: Police in Harvey, Ill., have arrested a woman and an auto mechanic on adultery charges after the woman's husband discovered them in bed together. Officers made the arrest to appease the cuckold, who otherwise "could have went off and done something crazy," Harvey Police Chief Phillip Hardiman said. The state is unlikely to win a conviction, observers say. Meanwhile, Dorothy Hutelmyer, 40, of Graham, N.C., has been awarded $1 million in damages from her husband's former secretary. Mrs. Hutelmyer said an affair between her husband and the woman destroyed the love and affection in her marriage, leading to divorce. Mr. Hutelmyer and the secretary are now married. North Carolina is one of the few states which still have "alienation of affection" laws on the books. Defense attorney Wayne Abernathy is appealing the award as excessive. "I think most lawyers think the law is extremely outdated," he said. (UPI, AP) *...Especially now that their ex-wives have heard about the verdict.*

Sayonara: A 35-year-old Japanese man sued his bride for 4.5 million yen (US$38,100) for not performing her wifely duties — cooking, cleaning and laundry. The woman, who has a full-time job, separated from her husband soon after their wedding when she learned of his demands, and they are now divorced. Tokyo District Court Judge Hiroto Waki threw out the suit, but ordered that the woman return her wedding ring to her ex-husband. (Reuters) *...But not until she can get a warning inscribed in it.*

Help, I've Fallen and I Can't Get Up: Abdel-Sattar Abdel-Salam Badawi was in the hospital in Menoufia, Egypt, and woke up to find himself in the hospital's morgue refrigerator. "I moved my hands and pushed [open] the coffin's lid to find myself among the dead," Badawi said. He shouted for help, but no one heard him through the sealed door. Twelve hours after he "died", three attendants found him when they went to the morgue to retrieve his body. "One of the employees fell dead" from the shock of finding him alive, Badawi said. (AP) *...What a loyal employee! He was clearly just ensuring the hospital's morgue count remained correct.*

Take Me To Your Leader: A psychologist at the Chillicothe (Ohio) Correctional Institution says virtually all the inmates he's talked to who claim they've been abducted by aliens describe them as having triangular faces with large eyes. "My estimation is that it's a universal thing. That face is a template ingrained into the brain back in the facial recognition area," Dr. Fred Malmstrom says. However, he remains incredulous of the inmates' stories. "Do I believe that they've been abducted [by aliens]? No." (UPI) *...More likely, they cracked their eyes open in the middle of a dream to find themselves nose-to-nose with a curious cat.*

Endangered Species: Actress Penny Marshall was hosting a fashion show for Kmart's Sesame Street line of clothing when she started to fall off the runway. She grabbed at Big Bird for support — and ripped off his right wing. The quick-thinking actor inside told the kids in the audience not to worry. "It'll grow back," he told them. Marshall was unhurt, but says she doubts she'll ever work with puppets again "now that I injured the bird." Meanwhile, an actor dressed as Barney the purple dinosaur filming an episode of the "Barney & Friends" TV show suffered smoke inhalation when a cooling fan in his 60-pound suit shorted out. Seeing something like that "can be really devastating to a 3-year-old," a show spokeswoman said. "They love Barney and they think that something terrible has happened to him." (AP, Reuters) *...Actually, it's the parents: they **hope** something terrible has happened to him.*

Run Over by Train, Florida Man Says Head Hurts
Reuters headline

Wildcat: The U.S. Fifth Circuit Court of Appeals in Texas has ordered a hearing to determine whether a trial should continue in Houston. Judge Kenneth Hoyt, presiding over a case of "environmental racism" relating to a Chevron oil facility from the 1920s, questioned whether a medical report should be accepted as evidence "because white people wrote it." The case, in which a "Negro neighborhood" was created on top of old Texas oil pits, cannot get a fair trial, Chevron says, after the judge said race was not a factor in determining whether residents were sickened by ground pollutants, ruling "It's not because they are black, but because they live in a certain area that white people put them in." To help explain his thoughts, transcripts show the judge theorized, "Why do you think Chinese people are so short? Because there is so much damn wind over there they need to be short.... It's environmental." Since that apparently wasn't clear enough, he lectured, "If you're seven feet tall and you're standing in China, then you're going to get blown away by that Siberian wind, aren't you?" (Reuters) *...Ya'know, Hoyt sounds like he's all hat and no cattle.*

Meet Your Neighbor, Ned: A Las Vegas builder has created a replica of the family house in "The Simpsons" animated TV series in their new Springfield subdivision. The house, which will be given away in a drawing, is as close a replica as possible, builder Kaufman & Broad said, right down to the furniture. The designers "spent hundreds of hours watching reruns" of the show to ensure the house was authentic. "Where else but in Vegas can you have a Pyramid, a replica of the New York skyline, and a home built from a cartoon?" asked a company spokesman. (Arizona Republic) *...That is unusual for Vegas, where most places are built from a movie — "House of the Damned".*

Searching for a Heart When in Need of a Brain: Twelve thieves broke into the Yunnan Tin Co. in Gejun, China, and stole so much tin that they needed four taxis to help haul it all away. The tin had been recovered from ore with help from arsenic, which forms a poison gas when exposed to water. It was raining during the theft. Eight of the gang are dead; two are in critical condition. (AFP) *...Just another case of natural deselection in action.*

Just Wanna Be Like You: Rock singer John Ford Coley called the Suffolk County (N.Y.) District Attorney to complain that a man was impersonating him, and even performing in concerts as him. Bruce Stelzer, 45, was arrested and charged with petit larceny, criminal impersonation and a scheme to defraud. It was reported that Stelzer got the idea when customers at a karaoke bar told him his Coley singing impression was "extraordinary". Meanwhile, a 12-year-old girl has been arrested by police in Lakewood, Colo. The girl allegedly dressed as a Girl Scout and sold snack items in several neighborhoods, but "Nobody got any candy or nuts," said detective Jim Greer. The girl has been charged with criminal impersonation and theft. (UPI, Denver Post) *...Hey, cut her some slack: that first felony merit badge is a tough one to get.*

Just Wanna Be Like You Too: When Robert Sullivan retired from teaching and got his first retirement check, he sent it back because it was twice as large as it should have been. An investigation of California state records revealed there were two Robert Sullivans teaching school, both using the same identification numbers, and both paying into the state teachers' retirement fund. Police say Willie Clifton Wright, 59, bought copies of Sullivan's teaching credentials, assumed his identity, and taught at Inglewood High School under Sullivan's name for 10 years. Wright was arrested but pleaded not guilty to five counts of perjury for applying for driver licenses under various names, two counts of impersonating Sullivan and one count of grand theft for collecting a salary for teaching. (UPI) *...If it was "theft" to take a teaching salary, does the school plan to recall 10 years' worth of diplomas?*

Debtor's Prison: "I couldn't believe it at first," said Darren Cooper of York, England. "I thought it was a joke." He had received a tax bill in the mail that threatened to take him to court if he didn't pay the balance within 14 days. The balance shown on the bill: one penny. He rushed to council offices to pay his debt immediately. At first, "I considered paying the penny by cheque so the council would have to wait seven days for it to clear," he said, but he had brought enough cash with him and used that instead. (Yorkshire Post) ... *"We don't pay taxes. Only the little people pay taxes."* *—American hotelier Leona Helmsley, before her imprisonment for tax evasion.*

Put Another Candle on the Birthday Cake: With the death of 122-year-old Jeanne Calmet, Marie-Louise Meilleur has been crowned the world's oldest person. Rita Gutzman, her 72-year-old daughter, says she plans to celebrate with a special party for Meilleur's 117th birthday. Not just any party: "We want it to be a surprise." Meanwhile, one of Meilleur's unfinished goals in life is to find a bride for her 81-year-old son, who lives with her in a nursing home. (AFP) ...*Some people just can't have enough grandchildren.*

Just Take Your Medicine Like a Man

Clinton Demands Children's Drug Dosages

UPI headline

Modern Family Values: Tracy Lee Whalin, 33, has been turned over to British custody after being charged in Florida with "lewd and lascivious behavior". Whalin left England with her son's 14-year-old best friend and was found with the boy in a Florida resort hotel. When police knocked on the door, he answered and said Whalin couldn't come to the door because "She's not decent right now." The woman has three children. Meanwhile, an 11-year-old boy is about to become Britain's youngest known father. The mother, his 15-year-old next-door neighbor, was reportedly shocked to discover he was only 11. Still, "I think he will be a good father. He may only be 11 but he is quite mature and responsible for his age." (Reuters, 2) ...*In other words, he sometimes gives her half of his milk money.*

Modern Family Values II: "We made a plan. The only way to keep us together was to have a baby," said a 14-year-old boy who got his school teacher pregnant when he was 13. Mary Kay LeTourneau, 35, a teacher at Shorewood Elementary School in Burien, Wash., met the boy when he was in the second grade. When her husband discovered what was going on he left, taking their four children. The boy's mother is bringing up the baby girl. LeTourneau has pleaded guilty to second-degree child rape and is facing seven years in prison. In an interview, she said her sexual relationship with the boy seemed "natural" to her. "What didn't seem natural was that there was a law forbidding such a natural thing." LeTourneau's "strict Catholic" father, former Republican Rep. John Schmitz of Orange County, Calif., was known for pulling his children out of school anytime there were sex education classes scheduled. He resigned in 1983 when it was revealed he had a mistress and two illegitimate children. (AP) ... *"What a man sows, that shall he and his relations reap." —Clarissa Graves (1892–1985), British poet.*

Rice is on Aisle 8: Feel like you're drowning in your marriage? Natalia and Ricardo have a head start: they were married 42 feet underwater in Spain's Bay of Biscay. Fighting a strong current, the couple, whose last name was withheld, signaled "I do" by signaling "thumbs up" to vows written on a board. Wetsuited witness Gonzalo Pineiro said the ceremony was "very moving". In Springfield, Mass., Dennis Lee and Clara Mae Ambra were wed in an aisle — a grocery aisle at the Big Y Supermarket — while shoppers parked their carts to watch. "He couldn't wait," Ambra said. "He's very romantic." (AFP, AP) ...*He shouldn't have rushed — if he had remembered to use his "double" coupon he could have married twins.*

Gray Lady Down: Calle has tuberculosis, but refuses to take her medicine. Calle, 30, an Asian elephant at the San Francisco Zoo, spat out her TB medicine even when it was hidden in cookies, bread, or sherbert. Zookeepers finally called in Berkeley pharmacist John Garcia, who specializes in concocting special medications. His prescription: two-pound cocoa butter suppositories. The medicine must be administered daily for two months, then three times a week for 10 months. It takes four handlers to administer each $800, ten-inch suppository. "It's not a pretty sight," a zoo spokeswoman said. (Bay City News) ...*Forget the $154,000 for the suppositories. How much do they have to pay the handlers?*

Boxers or Briefs? Inmates in the Linn County (Ore.) Jail liked to clog the pipes with their underwear, and one inmate even tried to hang himself with his briefs' waistband. So now, male inmates may no longer have underwear, though they will be allowed clean pants three times per week instead of twice. Only one prisoner has complained so far, Sheriff Dave Burright said. "He claimed it was an unquestionable constitutional right for inmates to have underwear," but "I don't remember Thomas Jefferson putting anything about underwear in the Constitution." Meanwhile, Ripley's Believe or Not museum in Los Angeles has reported that a pair of Elvis Presley's underwear has been stolen from a display. The custom made, black briefs "were specially designed with extra-strength elasticity to endure [Elvis'] stage antics and pelvic gyrations," a Ripley's spokesman said. However, "displays featuring a pair of Madonna's panties were untouched." (AP, 2) ...*Madonna touches her panties enough for everybody.*

Don't Touch That Dial: Chicago public radio station KBEZ's "Annoying Music" is such a success, it's going national. The three-minute radio show features strange songs that might not get played by other stations, such as Slim Whitman yodeling "It's a Small World". Jim Nayder, the program's creator, says that the "Small World" song "is annoying on its own, but this particular version was like a train wreck." Nayder makes a distinction between bad and annoying. "Bad music, you switch the station. Annoying music is sort of like passing an accident — you know you don't want to look, but you sort of have to." (AP) ...*Kind of like Madonna's panties.*

Workout: Latisha Wright, 11, was tired of waiting for her mother to finish her workout. Mom had left the keys in the car so Latisha and her cousin, Shakierra Mack, 8, could listen to the radio. When

Patricia Wright, 33, finished her workout, the car and the children were gone. Latisha drove the car 50 miles to visit her aunt in Lynchburg, Va. It was far enough away that she had to stop for gas. Latisha will not be charged, a police spokesman said, noting "I think her mother's going to punish her enough." Mrs. Wright was charged with child neglect. (AP) *...And, with enough of that police-approved punishment, she might also be charged with child abuse.*

Go Figure

FBI's 'Most Wanted' List Full of Fugitives

Reuters headline

Accentuate the Positive: Contrary to conventional wisdom, psychologists from the University of California in Berkeley and Catholic University in Washington, D.C., say laughter is the best way to get over grief when a loved one dies. In the past, it was thought that a person had to "work through" the stages of anger, sadness and depression after a death. "It may be that focusing on the negative aspects of bereavement is not the best idea because people who distanced themselves by laughing were actually doing better years later," one of the researchers said. "We found the more people focus on the negative, the worse off they seem later." (UPI) ... *"Either that wallpaper goes, or I do." —Oscar Wilde's last words.*

Tonic and Tonic: "Wander down the Strand in London and you will see the evidence. How many of the alcoholics are ever bald?" asks hair loss expert Dr. Hugh Rushton of the Institute of Trichologists in London. Rushton says bald men tend to have an excess of testosterone, but heavy drinkers damage their livers so much that it cannot process the hormone. Thus, if you find a man who is a heavy drinker, it is likely he'll still have his hair, Rushton said. (Reuters) *...Ah, but who cares when it's just the hair of the dog?*

Bash for Cash: Always alert for ways to keep people interested in the national lottery, Britain's lottery regulators have approved "TV Dreams", a show where contestants will engage in gladiator-style combat in a battle for $165,000 in lottery prize money. Those who cannot fight may choose a champion. The show will air on Saturdays in prime time. (AP) ...*Isn't that how the decline of ancient Rome started?*

Do I Know You, Dear? Forget your lover's name during sex? Russell Lane of the West London Neurosciences Center at Charing Cross Hospital says you can blame "transient global amnesia". Lane publicized the case study of a 64-year-old man who had multiple instances of "stereotyped attacks of amnesia after intercourse." The episodes lasted for 30 to 60 minutes, leaving the victim with "only a very hazy recollection of foreplay." (Reuters) ...*And if you forget your lover's name before sex, it's known as "normal dating behavior".*

Over Easy: Emu eggs shells are a powerful aphrodisiac, says Australian artist Ivan Durrant. Durrant carves the huge eggs of the six-foot, flightless, fast-running bird, and made his discovery by accident. "There was a lot of egg dust flying around and I happened to lick my fingers ... and, well, I was unstoppable," he claims, noting his friends have found similar results when they tried the magic dust. "About a quarter of a teaspoon of powdered emu egg shell is enough to get you randy for at least two days," he said. (AFP) ...*Nature is wonderful: it knows you need two days just to catch an emu.*

Herpetology Happenings: A Los Angeles woman has won $1500 in damages from Angus Johnson, the owner of a 7-foot boa constrictor named Alissss, after his snake slithered over to her patio and ate her 2-pound pet Chihuahua. Flossie Torgerson sued Johnson for the value of her dog, her emotional distress over witnessing the event, and the expenses of circulating a petition to outlaw pet snakes in residential neighborhoods. Meanwhile, the Newport, R.I., fire department was called to aid a woman who was visiting a friend's apartment. He had taken his two-foot Savannah monitor lizard out of its cage to it to show her when the animal grabbed her with its legs, bit her chest, and wouldn't let go. Unable to pry it off, a veterinarian injected the lizard with a sedative, which relaxed it enough that it could be pulled loose. "She was relatively calm from what I understand," a fire department spokesman said. (UPI, AP) ...*Sure: that was less horrifying than what she expected when the friend dragged her into his room to show her his "two-foot lizard".*

Handcuff Happenings: "You know I'm drunk. Just take me to jail," demanded Kellie Parini of the Butte, Mont., police officer that had pulled her over. Officer William Burt handcuffed Parini behind her back and put her in the back of his patrol car. While he was checking over her car, Parini allegedly was impatient at the delay, climbed into the front seat of the police cruiser, and drove off. Burt followed in Parini's car, but lost her. He found her when he got to the police station: she was sitting in his car in front of the station, waiting for him. In addition to drunk driving, she has been charged with criminal endangerment for allegedly trying to run Burt down, unauthorized use of a motor vehicle, and resisting arrest. (AP) ...*With time off for providing Burt a fun story to tell his grandchildren.*

Handcuff Happenings II: Police in Cologne, Germany, were called to the bedside of a 30-year-old man and his girlfriend after they had handcuffed themselves to the bed, then broken the key off in the lock. The officers "cut the handcuffs with a bolt cutter and then left quietly," reports said. (Reuters) ...*A clear case of police chivality.*

Stupid
Artificial Intelligence like Real Thing
UPI headline

Rats! The airport in Barranquilla, Colombia, was shut down for an hour after a power outage. Investigators found the problem: a rat short-circuited the airport's power grid when it urinated on an electrical junction. "The rat was quite frazzled," noted Civil

Aviation director Ramon Emiliani. Meanwhile, a rat has been implicated in the deaths of 14 hospital patients in San Pedro Sula, Honduras. The rodent chewed through electrical wiring, frying itself and cutting power to life support equipment. The deaths weren't discovered until hours later, however, because "The hospital has very few employees on the weekends," hospital Director Gustavo Zuniga explained. (Reuters, AP) ...*I didn't realize there were HMOs in Honduras.*

Fly Me: After an investigation, a British Airways 757 flight crew has been cleared of wrongdoing after the News of the World published a photograph taken by a reporter through the open cockpit door. It showed a 5-year-old girl sitting on the pilot's knee and allegedly pushing flight control buttons. "She didn't do a lot and she didn't really press any buttons," said the girl's father, Keith Pickersgill of Leeds, England. The girl had been invited to the cockpit to help her get over her fear of flying. (AP) ...*That accomplished, she now has a mortal fear of tabloid photographers.*

Storm Clouds: Like many towns, Harbor Springs, Mich., has a problem getting rid of all the sewage it generates. It has applied for a state permit to try something new: City Manager Fred Geuder wants to turn it into snow, adding to the 140 inches of white stuff the town already gets each winter from more natural sources. Using snow-making machines borrowed from a nearby ski resort, city officials plan to blow 80,000 gallons of wastewater into the air per day; the cold kills any bacteria, and the resulting snow settles back to the ground to await spring thawing, officials say. Geuder says the project is "really as exciting as this can get." (UPI) ...*If you think that's exciting, wait until you see what happens when voters find their kids eating their snowmen.*

King of the Asphalt Jungle: A six-year-old boy in Sweden still doesn't have a name. After his parents tried to register his name as "Brfxxccxxmnpckcccc111mmnprxvc1mnckssqlbb11116" (pronounced "Albin"), the government rejected the name registration and fined the parents 5,000 kronor (US$625), saying the name is unsuitable under Sweden's naming law [see *This is True: Glow-in-Dark Plants Could Help Farmers,* p 118]. The parents say the name is "a meaningful, expressionistic typographic formulation which we consider to be an artistic new creation in the pataphysical tradition in which we believe." Authorities rejected that argument, as well as the parent's most recent name suggestion, "A". Should the family choose to flee Sweden, they can: the boy has a passport. In it, his name is listed as "Boy Tarzan". (AFP) *...Probably relating to his agonizing, animalistic scream anytime he tries to spell his name.*

I Knew That: When Bill Clinton received a gift of a Romanian flag, he saw it had a big hole in the middle. The hole is symbolic: the Communist emblem that used to be in the middle of the banner had been hacked out to symbolize the 1989 revolt that brought the country to democracy. The confused president sent a note to Romania thanking them for the "poncho". White House spin doctors claimed the leader of the free world was merely "joking" with his "light-hearted comment". Meanwhile, according to a Gallup poll 53 percent of British citizens do not know the United States used to be a British colony. Just 40 percent demonstrated they knew the fact. (AP, 2) *...Apparently, the other seven percent think the U.S. is **still** a colony.*

Sacramental Whine: The Chama First Baptist Church in Santa Fe, N.M., has won their legal battle. A jury ruled the church was not liable for the actions of Louis Day, a former pastor, for alleged negligence in his marriage counseling of two church members. Pastor Day admitted he was regularly having sex with the female half of a married couple who came to him for counseling. The jury said church officials did enough by confronting Day when they learned of the affair, causing the married minister to resign his post. Day says he cannot remember how often he and the woman had sex inside the church. "I don't keep notches in my Bible to keep a record of such things," he testified. (Reuters) *...Then what do the notches signify? The number of parishioners he took behind the altar?*

Heavy Conscience: Ohio Wesleyan University has its clapper back. "I can finally live in peace. Do you know what it is like, carrying that thing around all these years?" read the anonymous note that accompanied it. The clapper, which weighs 40 pounds and was from the bell in the school's Gray Chapel, was stolen "decades" ago in a student prank. The negative reaction from other students at the time made the culprits afraid to come forward to return the bell's banger. (AP) ...*The cagey kleptomaniac collegians kept the copper clapper they copped in the closet, contrite but incapable of confessing until conditions cooled. Cowards!*

T.P. Phone Home

Dysfunctional Toilet
Phones Woman

AFP headline

Give Them a Foot and They'll Want a Mile: "It may look like a $100,000 foot," suggests San Francisco Mayor Willie Brown. Ridiculous, says artist Buster Simpson: it's a $400,000 foot. At issue is a sculpture Simpson is designing for the city's Embarcadero district, to be paid for by the San Francisco Art Commission. Simpson wants to sculpt a gigantic foot out of marble or granite, which would require the higher price tag, to symbolize "the motion of the foot embarking on land." When he heard that Brown thought it should cost less, Simpson scoffed. "Maybe if the mayor wants it in tin or something — or maybe inflatable," he suggested. (AP) ...*No no no. For it to be a proper monument to the mayor, it would have to be an inflatable head.*

After Careful Study: An investigation by Johns Hopkins University shows that only about ten percent of the adults who diagnose themselves as suffering from attention deficit disorder actually test positive for the malady. "ADD is a pretty rare condition, especially in adults," noted researcher Doug Johnson-Greene. (UPI) ...*If they'd simply paid attention to the research, they would have realized that.*

To Your Health: British vegetarians are aghast that several rural water plants are using charcoal made from cow bones to filter drinking water. The bones, from India, cannot carry the "mad cow" disease plaguing some domestic cows, Yorkshire Water says. It could be worse: the San Diego, Calif., Metropolitan Wastewater Department is ready to begin "pioneering a process ...to get people comfortable with the idea of drinking treated sewage," a spokesman says. The process would attach the outflow of sewage treatment plants to the inflow of local water reservoirs. (AP, UPI) ...*Hollywood has been using that process for years for its feature films.*

Train Reek: Train drivers in South Africa are complaining about how much passengers smoke. Or, perhaps more so, *what* they smoke: marijuana. "The drivers have been complaining for quite a while about dagga smoke, but the problem seems to be getting a lot worse," said a Metrorail spokeswoman. She says the railway is considering making the passenger car next to the driver non-smoking "and policing it strictly. It's either that or we install fans." (Reuters) ...*Or just asking passengers to stick their heads out the windows to exhale.*

Are they Live, or are they Mammorex? Norm Zadeh has a unique idea for his new topless photo magazine, "Perfect 10". Only women without breast implants may pose. He wants readers to remember "what real breasts look like, because they've forgotten. They think when a women lays down, her breasts are supposed to stand straight up, like rockets ready for launch." Magazine industry analyst Samir Husni of the University of Mississippi doesn't think Zadeh has much of a chance. "If he's going for the puritan at heart, he's wrong. The puritans aren't going to be looking at a naked woman in the first place." Husni says. "If it's a fantasy magazine, why do I want to look at something real?" (AP) ...*If men wanted plastic, they'd fantasize about Barbie.*

Same Song, Different Verse: Mattel, Inc., has sued MCA records over the song "Barbie Girl" by the Danish group Aqua. The song includes such lyrics as "Make me walk, make me talk / Do whatever you please / I can act like a star / I can beg on my knees." A Mattel spokesman says the song "represents a blatant and unauthorized use of our most valuable property," the Barbie doll. "It's a brand we have built over the past 38 years and we will do everything possible to protect its integrity." (AP) ...*Barbie's body is a temple; they merely want to prey.*

Ad Blitz: With the death of Princess Diana, the Wendy's restaurant chain has decided not to run a new ad in which company founder Dave Thomas asks customer Queen Elizabeth (played by a look-alike), "So, how're the kids?" And Weight Watchers has pulled a spot featuring the real-life Sarah Ferguson, the Duchess of York, who tells viewers that losing weight is "harder than outrunning the paparazzi." Both TV commercials were filmed before Diana's fatal car crash. Meanwhile, a newspaper advertisement run by police in Warsaw, Poland, a week after Diana's death features a photo of Diana and lamenting her "banal and absurd tragedy" to bring more attention to their anti-drunk driving campaign. Finally, a newspaper editor called a competing paper's decision to accept an ad from the Volvo car distributor in Macau "despicable". The advertisement features a photo of Diana and offers a "safety bonus" of 30,000 patacas (US$3,700) for each Volvo purchased. (various) ...*1997: the year people started wondering, "Why can't everyone be as sensitive to my feelings as corporate America?"*

Stinking Rich: A study by the University of California, Los Angeles, finds that the number-one criterion women use for picking a mate is the man's money-making ability. Men, on the other hand, are more likely to value a woman's physical attractiveness. However, men are starting to realize that their own good looks can help bring in women with better incomes. In other words, "men also recognize there is potential economic value in their looks," says researcher Saskia Karen Subramanian. At the same time, a study by the Institute of Urban Ethology in Vienna report that women like the smell of ugly men more than handsome men. Women smelled T-shirts worn by various men who had been rated as more or less good-looking. They liked the smells of the less-handsome men better. The results were the opposite of similar studies conducted with men sniffing women's shirts. (AP, AFP) ...*That's because the study of men used shirts that were still on the women.*

If We Have the Former, We Definitely Want the Latter
Flying Cars and Doggie Diapers: Do We Need Them?
Reuters headline

Car 54, Where Are You? Police in Recife, Brasilia, are suffering a shortage of police vehicles after state authorities seized most of the cars officers used to get around. They weren't theirs. "It was normal practice for detectives and inspectors to commandeer stolen cars and use them as if they were their own," said a spokesman for Pernambuco state security. Most affected were the officers assigned to the car theft detail — all 40 of their cars were confiscated in the raid. (Reuters) ...*Necessity is the mother of circumvention.*

This Won't Hurt a Bit: Hong Kong authorities are calling death rates in local hospitals "alarming". In recent incidents, hospital staffers have accidentally hooked up oxygen tubes or bottles of milk to IV lines, given patients blood of the wrong type, and removed a girl's fallopian tube thinking it was an inflamed appendix. Dr. Lee Kin-hung, president of the Hong Kong Medical Association, insists that bungling hasn't increased, it's just that more "attention is brought because of the headlines in the newspapers." But a Hong Kong legislator, who is also a doctor, insists the situation needs to improve: "The system should be foolproof so that even fools [working in the hospitals] can't kill people." (AP) ...*How about assigning them to the legislator's hospital for some special training?*

Underground Railroad: A "dead" 2-year-old girl from the village of Yakasse-Feyasse, Ivory Coast, was rescued from a grave after three days underground when cemetery workers digging a grave nearby heard her sighing. They dug her up and returned her to her parents. And in Craiova, Romania, a family was pressured into burying a boy even though they insisted the body wasn't their missing son. "Straight away we saw that it wasn't our son. But the police treated us as if we were heartless parents and forced us to say it was Claudiu," Mariana Novac said. After two months, Claudiu came home, and the parents are working to get his name off the death register so he can return to school. (Reuters, AFP) *...If all else fails, he can take the identity of the kid they buried.*

We've Got Sprits, We've Got Spirits, How 'bout You? "I just wanted to be able to wear my rosary beads to show my faith," complained a 15-year-old high school sophomore and Catholic altar boy. He had been prohibited from wearing his rosary at New Caney High School, north of Houston, Texas, because school administrators ruled the beads were "gang apparel". A federal judge disagreed and ordered the school to allow students to wear their religious symbols. (Reuters) *...Catholic garb is "gang apparel"? Next thing you know, some bureaucrat will claim Catholics and Protestants are terrorists bent on bombing each other to smither— ...uh, never mind.*

Sugar and Spice: Police in Hawaii say they have confiscated more than 1,900 tickets for a phony Spice Girls concert. Investigators say John Lewis, also known as Akram Abdullah-Wasi, was arrested after he sold the tickets in a scam to help pay for a sex change operation. (AP) *...So much for his plans to become the newest Spice Girl, "Onion". Peel her and it brings tears to your eyes.*

Peak Perfection: Maps have long indicated that northern Germany's highest mountain, the Brocken, was 1,142 meters (3,747 feet) high. But more accurate recent measurements showed it was only 1,140 meters. Rather than force a change in maps, a construction company trucked 19 tonnes of granite to the peak, stacking the rocks in a two-meter-high pile. (AFP) *...There they go again, making a mountain out of a molehill.*

Home Run: A woman is suing the Chicago Cubs for $50,000 because, she says, a security camera at Wrigley Field is pointed at her bedroom window, allowing peeping stadium security guards to invade her privacy. She says stadium officials assure her that the camera is merely monitoring the activities of nearby police officers. But, Susie Nelson counters, "I never noticed there being any police activity in my bedroom." (UPI) ...*Stadium security could probably arrange that, if you're ever in the mood.*

Please Don't Squeeze the Charmin: Britain's Advertising Standards Authority has upheld complaints against a Citroen advertisement which described the car as "positively sphincter twitching." They note that in the ad, "the inclusion of the toilet paper implied that people could drive so fast or so dangerously that they or their passengers could lose control of their bowels." The ASA has asked for the ad to be withdrawn, warning "speed and acceleration should not be the predominant message of an advertisement." Separately, the Independent Television Commission in London has given an OK to a deodorant ad. The spot is set in a nude drawing class filled with female students in which "it is made clear" that the male model "has become sexually aroused." The ITC said a voluntary restriction that the ad could not be shown before 9:00 p.m. was sufficient "for the level of innuendo contained in the commercial" and that "the imagery [did not go] beyond the bounds of general good taste." (Reuters, AFP) ...*Innuendo OK, outuendo not OK.*

"Gimme that Back!" Growls an Outraged Jessie Helms

Newt Gingrich Finds Dinosaur Bone

AP headline

Final Exit, Part I: When several young women complained to soldiers near a swimming pool in Nsele, Congo, that they had been groped by men in the water, the soldiers figured the best way to get the more than 100 people in the pool to stop swimming and pay attention to them was to fire their rifles into the air. Bad idea: at least 18 swimmers drowned in the resulting panic. (AP) ...*Getting their attention was as easy as shooting fish in a barrel.*

Final Exit, Part II: Shannan Thompson, 16, needed to fix her hair. Since she was driving along Interstate 95 near Fellsmere, Fla., at the time, she asked a passenger to take the wheel while she primped. He lost control and the car flipped over. Two of the four teens inside, including the wheel man, were killed; the others, including Thompson, were seriously injured. (AP) ...*It was just so senseless: that guy on the motorcycle wasn't even a photographer.*

Final Exit, Part III: Cook County (Ill.) Juvenile Court Judge Richard Walsh is defending his sentence of a 16-year-old girl who beat her father to death with a baseball bat. In a plea bargain, she agreed to drop an insanity defense to first degree murder charges and pleaded guilty to second-degree murder. The judge apparently believed her allegations that her father was molesting her, even though prosecutors said there was no evidence to support the girl's claims, so he sentenced her to just five years probation so she could return to her high school honors classes. He noted that "if there's anything to be learned from this, it's that if you mess with your kids, they are going to beat your brains in." (AP) ...*Those who can, do. Those who can't, teach. Those who can't learn, judge.*

Great Escapes I: Police finally caught up to Jason Duhagon, 26, after an hour-long chase. "We tried to stop the guy for a routine traffic violation," a Danville, Calif., police spokesman said. "He may not even have gotten a ticket." During the chase, Duhagon tossed rubber gloves and several Halloween masks out his window. Police charged him with reckless driving, resisting arrest ...and littering. (Marin Independent Journal) ...*Want to wager which of the charges results in the biggest fine in California?*

Great Escapes II: When Judge Mark Atkinson revoked Mark Conover's bail for showing up late to a Houston, Tex., court appearance for driving with a suspended license, Conover made a run for it. He sprinted down a hallway with the bailiff in hot pursuit, and was confronted by three doors: he chose Door Number 3. Bad choice: door 1 was the stairway, his route out of the building; door 2 was another courtroom; door 3 led to holding cells. "He was embarrassed" by his choice, the bailiff said. Conover now faces a felony escape charge and a possible 25-year prison sentence. (Houston Chronicle) ...*Or you can take the* *punishment behind Curtain Number 2 where Carol Merrill is standing.*

Great Escapes III: A helicopter crashed and burst into flames as it attempted to land in the yard of the prison in Sittard, Netherlands, killing the pilot and injuring the prisoner trying to escape in the copter. A prison spokesman said the crash resulted from the pilot hitting a pole erected in the yard to prevent helicopter escapes. (AFP) *...Warden, the bad news is there's a smoldering wreckage in the exercise yard. The good news is your "Chopper Stopper" works great!*

Campaign Launch: Now that astronaut Jerry Linenger is retiring from NASA, he is being courted to run for Congress against 10-term Representative David Bonior of Michigan. A spokesman for Michigan Gov. John Engler says Linenger has "a ton of attractive qualifications." (UPI) *...Which just shows the governor's ignorance: in space, Linenger proved to be as weighty as a feather.*

Iran Down the Aisle: An Iranian woman was so afraid that her best friend might get married and move away that she petitioned in court for permission for her husband to take the woman as his second wife. She said she was convinced that her friend would be "a companion at home, not a rival." The court granted the request. Meanwhile, a man in Mashhad, Iran, "faked a crime" in order to be thrown in jail in a scheme to marry his girlfriend. His idea was to gain the confidence of the girl's father, who was serving time in the same prison on drug charges. "I washed his clothes and cleaned his cell for several months, and managed to establish a friendly tie with him," said the lovestruck lad, identified only as Ahmad. "After gaining his confidence, I raised the issue [of marrying his daughter]. He first opposed the idea, but when I told him the story, he laughed and said 'what love can do to some people'," Ahmad said. Ahmad was released from prison; the father of the bride got a two-day pass to attend the wedding. (AFP, 2) *...In U.S. prisons, one is considered married within hours of being assigned a cell.*

It Was Inevitable the Top Brass Would
Blame the Female Recruits
Study Finds Broad
Problems in Army
AP headline

Disappearing Act: When magician David Copperfield toured Russia recently, a Russian Orthodox priest told people to stay away from the shows. "Even your presence as spectators during such occult performances has spiritual and physical consequences that can lead to madness and suicide," warned Father Tikhon, the head of the Sretenskiyi monastery in Moscow. Now that the tour is finished, someone is, indeed, mad — the government, which is downright angry. The tour's Russian promoters disbanded their company before paying any taxes on their $3 million profit. Russian Tax Police went to the Palace of Congresses in Moscow, where Copperfield performed, but the state-owned theater would not allow officers to take any records as evidence. "Under normal circumstances we could seize documents by force," a police spokesman said. "But storming the Kremlin would be too much." (AFP, Christian Science Monitor) *...Leading to the U.S.'s Internal Revenue Service calling the Russian Tax Police "pansies".*

Hi Ho, Hi Ho, We Hate the Gays You Know: "We want Mickey to come home," said one of the protesters outside the Walt Disney Studios in Burbank, Calif. "We don't want him to have a dress when he gets here." The group was demonstrating against Disney's "pro-homosexual policies" — health benefits for same-sex partners of employees. Disney employees at the studio reacted by giving the protesters water, soft drinks and cookies: it was 100 degrees in the parking lot. A Disney spokesman noted that the company is committed to "values that include tolerance and compassion and respect for everybody." (AP) *...Even, apparently, bigots.*

Oh, By the Way: September 5th was designated National Be Late For Something Day by the Procrastinators Club of America. The day was set aside for the chronically unpunctual, and to encourage others to consider not taking their schedules too seriously. "If you're not in the habit of procrastinating, this might be the one day to just try it out and see if you like it," Chief Procrastinator Les Waas told reporters — before September 5th. The club has 14,000 official members, but claims "at least half the human race" are unofficial members. (Reuters) ...*What, you honestly expected to hear about this earlier?*

Chew on This: A man in Taormina, Italy, had five and a half pounds of "inedible matter" removed from his stomach. Surgeon Vincenzo Morici removed 46 teaspoons, two cigarette lighters, a pair of tongs, and various other metal and plastic items from the "psychologically disturbed" man. "This is so extraordinary that I am going to present the case to the scientific community," Morici said. (AFP) ...*Just as soon as he's finished unloading at the pawn shop.*

Notice: Gate Locked, Enter through Hole in Fence: Agents from the U.S. Immigration and Naturalization Service raided a top-secret lab at Sandia National Laboratory in Albuquerque, N.M., and arrested 16 undocumented Mexican workers, the INS announced. The INS said the workers were repairing the roof of the nuclear weapons research facility. "It's such a high security area, the [military police] had trouble getting in," claimed the INS agent in charge. (Reuters) ...*Surely that makes the world feel much safer.*

404 — Intelligence Not Found: A City of Warren, Mich., public librarian has filed a grievance against Warren City Councilwoman Gloria Sankuer, who demanded that the librarian show her how to find "naked pictures" on the Internet. The librarian insisted she could not do that, since a local ordinance — written by Sankuer — made that illegal. "My need was urgent. I needed pictures of this disgusting, appalling porno on the Internet," Sankuer said later. The grievance says Sankuer became angry, and "berated" and raised her voice against the unnamed librarian. (Detroit Free Press) ...*See? Pornography doesn't lead to violence toward women. The lack of it does.*

House Call: A man came into Dr. Lui Siu-ko's Hong Kong clinic saying he worked with the "triad" gang. He told the doctor the clinic was in his district and demanded protection money. When Lui paid the HK$400 (US$50) fee, he asked for a receipt. Chan Koon Shing, 46, not only provided a receipt, it included his name and ID card number. The gangster was arrested, convicted and sentenced to prison within a week of his extortion attempt. (Reuters) *...Where, no doubt, other members of the triad will educate him in the finer points of maintaining a proper corporate image.*

Slam Drunk: Gary Sledzik, 44, of Webster, Mass., admits he was drunk. He does not contest that he was speeding, nor that he crashed his truck into a car, killing a 36-year-old woman and her 13-year-old daughter. But that has not stopped him from filing a claim against the state police for $300,000, saying they are at least partly at fault for the crash. Why? The claim alleges police failed to respond "promptly" to calls that Sledzik's truck was seen speeding. Sledzik's lawyer says the claim will be useful in civil court should the victims' family sue him for damages. (UPI) *..."No matter how cynical you get, you can't keep up." —Lily Tomlin.*

Panacea

Doctor Fixes Problem
by Severing Head
AP headline

That Sinking Feeling: The group Raise the Gunboat spent eight years collecting $220,000 in donations to raise a Civil War gunboat from the bottom of the Tennessee River. But now that Stephen James, an archaeologist with Panamerica Maritime of Memphis, has dived to the sunken boat, the group is rethinking its plans. The wreck is a barge, built at least 10 years after the end of the Civil War, James says. "They are good guys, but not archaeologists." The group is undeterred. "We think we know where [a gunboat] is," says State Rep. John Tidwell, a spokesman for the group. "We'll probably raise this boat for the structural value while we're trying to locate the Key West. Sort of a shakedown cruise." (AP) *...Just like a politician: if all else fails, call for a shakedown.*

Board on the Beat: Police in Serravalle, Italy, have a new weapon against crime: wooden policemen. Mayor Gianluca Buonanno got the idea at a play, which featured a wooden replica of himself as a prop. "Between the first and the second act, I swapped places with the dummy and for a few seconds nobody noticed," the mayor said. He hopes putting up decoy police officers will slow down speeders. (Reuters) *...We tried putting a wooden vice president in the White House, but it sure didn't reduce crime there.*

It's Academic: A judge has awarded Pamela Phelps, 23, 46,000 pounds (US$73,000) in her suit against the Hillingdon Borough Council outside London. She said Council schools failed to notice she was dyslexic, and the resulting poor education she received condemned her to a life of poorly paying jobs. (AP) *...Just sign here, ma'am, and we'll give you this check for 000,46 pounds.*

Take it in the Shorts: Belgian film director Jan Bucquoy needed financing for his next film, so he solicited underwear from "500 famous Flemish men" to help. The used undies will be auctioned off and the proceeds will go toward Bucquoy's movie, which is about the closing of a car plant, not shorts. Many of the celebrities sent in their underpants as requested. Except politicians, Bucquoy said. (AFP) *...They didn't want the answer to the infamous "boxers or briefs?" question to be made public.*

I Protest: Aundra Akins, 18, thought the 27-year sentence he received for his role in the Florida robbery of two British tourists that left one dead was a bit harsh, so he appealed based on a technicality. A jury convicted him again in the retrial, and the judge indeed thought a 27-year sentence was not altogether fair. Given the chance to rectify the injustice, he sentenced Akins to life. (AP) *...When you're a squeaky wheel, sometimes the best you can hope for is grease.*

Updated Driver Required — Insert CD in Dash: Microsoft Vice President Paul Maritz says that by the 1999 model year, automobiles might run software based on Microsoft Windows. He suggests people's cars will remember drivers' address books and schedules, and even "read" e-mail to the driver while going down the road. "You've got to keep your eyes on the road and your hands on the wheel," Maritz said, but "it's well within the realm of current technology." (Reuters) *...Just what we need: extremely cheap cars that crash and burn without cause or warning.*

Side B: After a long string of top-selling pop albums, Billy Joel says he is tired of rock music. "When I got to be 13, this hot seductress in shredded fishnet stockings swept me away: I had a passionate affair with rock 'n' roll," Joel says, noting he's ready to go back to his first love, classical music. "The boomers are out of the pop field right now. They don't like what they're hearing, and they're not buying it." (AP) *...Everybody's talkin' 'bout the new sound / Funny but it's still rock 'n' roll to me.*

Danger Signal: Erfat Seyyed Raggab wanted his friend Seyyed Lotfi Seyyed to quit smoking. Seyyed, a Cairo baker, is a long-time chain smoker. When Raggab, a plumber, started haranguing him again on the subject, Seyyed smashed a bottle and used the shards to stab Raggab to death. (AFP) *...Warning: incessant nagging may be dangerous to your health.*

Hand Cancel: Linda Worrall, a mail sorter for New Zealand Post, suffers from arachnophobia — an unnatural fear of spiders. So she doesn't think much of the country's new stamp series, "Creepy Crawlies", which features a katipo, a poisonous spider. Now, whenever she sees a letter with the spider stamp, she goes into a panic. "It's something that could come off the page, which I know sounds silly," Worrall says. "It's hard for people to understand, but it's so real." NZ Post is paying for counseling. (AP) *...If she wants to keep her job she'd better lick the problem.*

Please Leave Your Threat at the Sound of the Beep: Robert Lirette apparently was unhappy that his wife got a speeding ticket. The Houma, La., man left a phone message at the district attorney's office, saying he would "buy some guns and go to [the state police] and take care of business" rather than pay the ticket, prosecutors say. He also allegedly called the governor's mansion to say that he would "get an airplane and crash it into the governor's mansion." It wasn't hard to track Lirette down: he left his name and phone number both times. He was booked into the Terrebonne Parish Jail on three counts of felony intimidation. Lirette's wife had no comment. (AP) ...*Or, at least when she does make a comment, she doesn't include her name and phone number.*

Buzz Off

Human Version of
Fly Gene Found
AP headline

Absolut Architectur: A new building for an insurance company in Des Moines, Iowa, looks like the advertisements for Absolut vodka when lighted at night. "We wanted to make an impact, but this was not what we had in mind," said a spokesman for EMC Insurance. "There was some surprise ...as the building came together." A spokesman for the architect said the resemblance was not intentional, but Richard Lewis, who runs the Absolut account for TBWA Chiat/Day advertising in New York, isn't so sure. "I'm convinced the architect has this unconscious relationship with Absolut," Lewis said. "Once you have Absolut on the brain it shows up all over the place." (AP) ...*Mangled car wrecks, the Betty Ford Clinic, blood stains, puddles of vomit....*

How Say You: The Toronto jury for the trial of Howard Burke, accused of attempted murder, was ready to report its finding to the court. "I wanted to be very clear because I've never said anything so important," the jury foreman said later. "I cleared my throat, then I rose to speak, then I cleared my throat again just as I was about to say 'guilty as charged'." The judge, however, released Burke, leading the jurors to ask why. The judge heard the sound of the foreman's throat-clearing as "not" and thought the jury had acquitted the prisoner. Burke later turned himself in, saying he intends to prove that the jury really did intend to find him not guilty. (UPI) *...Caution: This verdict void where prohibited by law. Not responsible for errors or omissions. Your mileage may vary.*

Your Mileage May Vary II: Driving on the Nevada desert, British fighter pilot Andy Green got his jet-powered car up to 764.2 mph to be the first person to break the sound barrier on the ground. "Unlike what I've read in a lot of the newspapers, the car doesn't leap in the air and explode, I was delighted to find out," Green said. (Reuters) *...However, for some reason he couldn't hear his stereo once he got up to speed.*

Suburban Renewal: "Dude, I'm sorry I stole your building," an anonymous caller told Pete Maynard. Maynard had been discombobulated when he arrived at the Aurora, Colo., site of the 3,000-square-foot building he was preparing to move to his ranch to rebuild as a barn, and found the structure was missing. "The guy was actually crying on the phone," Maynard said. "I guess he felt remorseful or scared that the theft had gotten so much attention." The caller told Maynard, who had spent two months taking the building apart by removing 10,000 screws, where he could find the disassembled pieces. (Denver Post) *...Proving Maynard can, indeed, find the broad side of a barn.*

Cycle of Life: Police let a woman in Carmarthen, Wales, go with a warning after they found her riding her bicycle at 70 kph in a 50 kph zone. Ros Jones, a finalist in a local "slimmer of the year" competition, explained, "I had no idea I was going so fast. I have been cycling to lose weight and I suppose as I got fitter my speed has crept up." Meanwhile, Anthony Adams, 24, is refusing to pay a 120-pound (US$190) fine after police in Cambridge, England, stopped him for pedaling "furiously" on his bicycle in the city center at midnight. "He did in a public place drive or ride furiously to the annoyance, obstruction or danger of any resident or passenger," a magistrate found. Adams says he is in training for an attempt to break the record for cycling the longest distance in one hour. (AFP, 2) *... "It is a tale / Told by an idiot, full of sound and fury / Signifying nothing." —Shakespeare (Macbeth, act 5).*

Cycle of Life II: A bicyclist crossing an airport runway in Soro-caba, Sao Paulo, Brazil, was killed when he was hit by a landing airplane. Marcelo Dias dos Santos, 25, could not hear the plane coming because he was listening to his Walkman on headphones, investigators said. (Reuters) ...*No doubt he ran with scissors when he was younger, too.*

Wigged Out: Customs inspectors in Vienna thought the carefully piled-up hair of a woman arriving from Amsterdam looked sus-picious, but she refused to submit to a search because she had "spent just too much time and money" making it look nice. But the Austrian officials insisted, and found her head was shaved; the hair was a hollowed-out wig containing half a kilogram of heroin. Meanwhile, Rabbi Ovadia Yosef, spiritual leader of Is-rael's Shas political party, said that women who wear wigs will be damned. "If the woman wishes for righteous children, let her remove the wig, if not she shall have impertinent children," he warned. Worse, "both she and her wig will be burned in hell." (AFP, AP) ...*Gives new meaning to "bad hair day".*

Weighting to Inhale: When actress Ellia English was called to read for the role of Gloria in the film "Waiting To Exhale", she really got into the part: she gained 70 pounds to more accurately reflect the character's description. "The horrible part is I had just lost a great deal of weight," English said. "At audition time I'd gained only 40 pounds. But right after the audition the other 30 pounds came on almost immediately." It didn't help: "The part of Gloria went to Loretta Devine," she said. "It was heart-break-ing for me, but I was happy for Loretta. I've got to hand it to her. She was good. Her hips were a lot bigger than mine." (UPI) ...*You just can't fake that kind of talent.*

Unreal Estate: A man preparing a lot in Voronezh, Russia, to build a house found a rusting 550-pound aerial bomb from World War II buried eight feet underground. Disposal experts said the bomb had to be detonated in place, since it was too decayed to be moved safely. (AP) ...*Excellent! An instant basement.*

Two Out of Three Ain't Bad
One in Three UK Girls Regret Drunken Sex —Poll
Reuters headline

The Defense Wrests: An argument between Cuyahoga County (Ohio) Assistant Prosecutor Thomas Cahill and defense attorney Willie Griffin spilled from a courtroom and into a hallway at the County Justice Center. A witness said Cahill tried to walk away, but when police arrived Griffin had Cahill in a headlock and was punching him. The defense attorney reportedly says the prosecutor was the aggressor and complained, "[Cahill] broke my fist." (Plain Dealer) *...Certainly: a lawyer's mouth is the hardest part of his body.*

Pink Slip: Think your boss is tough? Then you're a pansy: a survey of Japanese civil servants asked, who would be an "ideal" boss? Second place, with only two-thirds the number of votes of the winner, was the manager of the Orix BlueWave, a baseball team that won the 1995 Japanese championship. Prime Minister Ryutaro Hashimoto took ninth place. The winner, by far? Mongol conqueror Genghis Khan. (AP) *...When he fired you, it was from a cannon.*

Lamentable Lawsuit: "At one point, all three women pulled the plaintiff's pants to his knees and caused him to fall," claimed a suit against Sterile Reprocessing Services, a Houston, Texas, medical supply company. "While struggling to get away, they dragged him across the floor by his pants." The victim, an unidentified man who was not wearing underwear, says that after the incident women at the plant would call him "Pee Wee" and "Shorty". He did not report the incident for two years, but the company settled for an undisclosed sum after the suit was filed. "The minute it was brought to the company's attention, they bent over backwards to help the kid," the company's attorney said. (Houston Chronicle) *...Wasn't "bending over backwards" what he was complaining about in the first place?*

Lamentable Lawsuit II: A U.S. District Court judge dismissed a lawsuit filed by Lt. Ed Wagner of the West Palm Beach (Fla.) Police Department after a fellow SWAT Team member gave him "noogies". Wagner claims the aggressive head rubbing aggravated an old neck injury. When he reported that, he was removed from the SWAT Team by the police chief, who noted "Anyone who has an easily injured neck has the potential to do additional damage and may be ineffective and a detriment to the team." The judge said the Americans With Disabilities Act does not apply to the case, since Wagner did not lose his job, just his duty assignment. (AP) *...Too bad it wasn't a "melvin", which may have qualified as sexual harassment.*

Lamentable Lawsuit III: "It's just unbelievable to me," said Jane Prejean, 79, of Fayetteville, N.Y. "He said, 'I'm going to sue you if you take away the money.' I just laughed. And he sued me." The "he" is James Prejean, 49, her son. James says he promised to love his mother, but that was based on her promise to support him for the rest of his life. She said she cut off his financial support to force him to get help for his "chronic alcoholism". State Supreme Court Justice Charles T. Major dismissed James' claim, ruling "a promise of love was not sufficient to establish the financial relationship as a contract." (AP) *...Although a three-martini power lunch would have been.*

Lamentable Lawsuit IV: A federal jury has awarded Capt. Tammy S. Blakey of Arlington, Wash., $875,000 in damages against Continental Airlines because the carrier did not protect her from sexual harassment in her airplane. Blakey says her mostly male co-workers would leave "raunchy surprises in the cockpit," such as pictures of naked women between the pages in flight manuals or pasted behind instrument panels. (Wall Street Journal) *...In addition to the $875,000, Continental is no longer allowed to call the little room in the front of the plane a "cockpit".*

Airline Antics II: A pilot and two of his crew have been "severely punished" by KLM Royal Dutch Airlines after a photographer took a picture of the three dancing on the roof of their 747 jet during a stop in Guatemala. The photo was published in newspapers all over the world, which is how KLM found out about the incident. The pilot was suspended for a week; the women's punishment was not announced, but "it was made clear to the crew that such actions are not permitted," KLM said. (AFP) ...*The Cha-Cha is not a sanctioned dance, even when the crew is in South America.*

Marlboro Man: Edward DeHart, a tobacco industry consultant who helped write the first "Surgeon General's Warning" on the side of cigarette packs, has died. He smoked until 1987, when doctors removed parts of his lungs in an attempt to stop his lung cancer. They failed. (AP) ...*Contrary to popular belief, "except me" is not part of that warning.*

RSVP: Researchers at a population control conference in Beijing were stunned to hear an academic from Ghana suggest that most family planning researchers forget to quiz one important demographic: the dead. Philip Adongo said he didn't forget: he interviewed them with the help of soothsayers. "If I only heard from the living, I wouldn't get a very good balance," he explained. (Reuters) ...*Most researchers still think he's unbalanced.*

And Darn It, Why Should It?
Stabbing Doesn't Spoil Friendship
AP headline

If You Can Read This Thank a Politician: A plan by India's Prime Minister Inder Kumar Gujral to reduce the country's nearly 50 percent illiteracy rate is being called "unworkable" by Mustaq Ahmed, chairman of the government-funded National Institute of Adult Education. Gujral's plan was to require students to prove they taught five people the alphabet before they would be allowed to graduate high school. But Ahmed says the plan would merely lead to a black market of forged completion certificates. Indian politicians are trying to figure out a new, more workable plan. (AFP) ...*Illiterate? Write for free help: GPO Box 5150, New Delhi.*

Up a Tree: A 35-year-old man in Madhya Pradesh, India, identified only as Nanku, thought his wife was unfaithful to him, so he "quit terra firma" and vowed to live in a tree "for the rest of his life." He lasted eight months before falling to his death. Meanwhile, Michelle Tribout was tired of her three children's whining. Her son Joseph, 13, said he was "really shocked" and didn't think "it would go this far" when Tribout, 36, escaped to the kids' tree house in the back yard, posting a sign declaring she was "On Strike". Daughter Rachel, 7, declared her mom "is pretty weird." Mom agreed to come down only after the kids promised to "pitch in when things need to be done and don't smart off," Joseph said. (AFP, UPI) ... *The headline: "Exasperated Mother Calls Whine, Won One".*

Free Market: "As long as they have lice, presumed criminals cannot be sent to prison, but must be looked after at the police station," says a police doctor in Prahova county, Romania. The policy has of course led to a "thriving trade in lice" among criminals, with suspects doing whatever they can to infest themselves when they are arrested. "While they are detained here, they get three meals and two snacks daily, as well as free medical treatment, which is hardly the case in prisons," said the doctor, who provides the medical care at state expense. (AFP) ... *Interesting to see how capitalism and socialism can sometimes work quite well together.*

Funny Money: Employees at Komercni Banka in Jablonec, Czechoslovakia, were counting the day's cash deposits when they stopped on a 1,000 crown (US$30) bill. Instead of a legend reading "Forging of notes will be prosecuted in accordance with the law," the notice proclaimed "This note is fake." It was otherwise "well forged," officials said. (Reuters) ... *Just because a guy has a good sense of humor doesn't mean he doesn't have a strong work ethic.*

Funny Money II: Now that the newly designed $100 bills are in circulation, the U.S. Treasury Department's Bureau of Engraving and Printing is ready to release their newly designed $50 bills. Except that the portrait of Ulysses S. Grant on 217.6 million of the notes printed so far have unacceptable flaws: Grant's hair looks funny. Since the way the hair is depicted is part of the bill's anti-counterfeiting protection, Treasury is planning to destroy and reprint the notes, which will cost taxpayers $7.6 million. (Reuters) ...*This "Bad Hair Day" thing is getting out of hand.*

And Now This: British newsreader Peter Rowell was preparing to go on the air on HTV West television to read the morning news bulletins while the station showed file footage of Princess Diana in a low-cut dress. "She had huge knockers!" Rowell enthused. His remarks went over the air; the station is considering disciplinary action. "Peter is absolutely distraught," an HTV spokesman said. "He made a comment which, because of unfortunate juxtaposition, could well have been badly interpreted." (AFP) ...*Clear proof that television executives consider viewers stupid.*

Cleaning Up This Town: A barking Yorkshire terrier chasing a street sweeping machine in Swansea, Wales, got too close and was sucked into the machine. Its owners, who apparently watched the entire incident, stopped the sweeper and recovered their dog unharmed. Meanwhile, police in Orlando, Fla., had just completed an 18-day effort to "clear" homeless people sleeping in the streets when a city sweeper accidentally swept up a man who, police say, had apparently been drinking and passed out in the gutter. He did not survive. (AFP, AP) ...*Things are rough when "living like a dog" is far beyond your dreams.*

Jurisprudence: When judges die in Oakland County, Mich., the county erects a memorial plaque at the courthouse. Circuit Court Judge William J. Beer is no exception, the Court Administrator says, because "it's inappropriate to pick and choose." Beer was forced out of office in 1983 when it was revealed that he lived weekdays with his wife and three sons, and weekends with a mistress and their nine children. The plaque notes Beer was "a true gentleman and distinguished jurist" who "loved literature and classical music. But above all, he loved the law." (UPI) ...*Actions speak louder than words.*

Batteries Not Included: Naoharu Yamashina, the founder of Japan's Bandai Co., has died. Bandai is best known for its Tamagotchi ("cute little egg") games. The company has sold more than 21 million of the "virtual pet" toys, mostly to children. (AP) ...*Damn it, we made it clear you have to feed him every day! Go to your room.*

Looks 10 Storeys Tall, Really Only Four

Phallus Museum Erected
in Reykjavik

AFP headline

Emergency Exit: Fred Nolan Jr. may be a thief, but he's not a petty thief. He was arrested in Spokane, Wash., on burglary charges, but he escaped from the police station. Apparently not having a use for the handcuffs he was wearing at the time, he mailed them back to the police department. "Unfortunately, the envelope had no return address," a police spokesman noted. (AP) ...*Try "Care of Penn and Teller, Las Vegas, Nevada."*

If You Believe This, It's a Miracle: Italian police, working to crack down on welfare fraud, came across a man who was registered as blind, yet held a driver's license. The unidentified man was arrested, but explained to a judge in Perugia that he had gone on a pilgrimage to Lourdes, France, last year and had his vision restored in a "miracle". The judge dismissed fraud charges against him. (Reuters) ...*The miracle is he was able to find such a gullible judge.*

Believe it or Not II: The Saybrook, Ill., Lions Club apparently liked 14-year-old Virginia Payne's Halloween costume. The girl was dressed in a white robe decorated with swastikas and phrases such as "Kill Them All" and "White Power" for the club's 35th annual costume contest. The Lions liked it so much, in fact, they awarded the eighth grader first prize. In the uproar that followed, Payne pointed out that she had a teardrop painted on her cheek to represent "the pain and suffering people endured during World War II." Further, "I didn't go [dressed] as a Nazi," she explained. "I went as a dead Nazi." (UPI, AP) ...*Please tell us she's going to flunk eighth grade. Please.*

Lights, Vanna, Action! Raymond Taylor did well on "Wheel of Fortune" — he won $81,000 in cash and prizes when he appeared on the game show in 1993. He liked it so much, "I wanted to have a life with the show," he says. "I loved the show enough to be a part of it." But the show didn't love him back: they say Taylor "stalked" the set and wouldn't leave, according to a lawsuit demanding that Taylor stay away from the production. "They feel like they have a relationship because they were treated so special the day of the show," says producer Marki Costello. "They don't realize that when we're done with them, we're done with them." (AP) ...*That's the Hollywood Way.*

I Spy: Poland's intelligence chief General Andrzej Kapkowski has issued new work rules for the country's spies. Cloak and dagger employees will be required to work only 40 hours per week, Monday through Friday, from 8:15 a.m. to 4:15 p.m. If weekend work is required, the trench-coated tradesmen must be given time off during the week in compensation. Further, pregnant spies must not be made to work more than eight hours per day, agents can only be put "on call" from home four times per month, and anyone who has to work surveillance missions in bad weather may go home two hours early. (AFP) ...*Also known as the "Come in from the Cold" rule.*

Object Lessons: A driving teacher from Carrington Middle School in Durham, N.C., was teaching two girls how to drive when they were allegedly cut off by another car. Police say instructor David Cline told the student driver to chase the car. When they caught up, Cline punched its driver in the nose. The victim took off, with the student vehicle again in hot pursuit. Police pulled them over for speeding, and the bleeding man told the officer what had happened. Cline was charged with assault; the student driver was not ticketed. Meanwhile, Duluth (Ga.) Middle School band teacher Johnny Broughton was arrested over the theft of more than $43,000 worth of band instruments. School officials did not notice the thefts because Broughton, who has been teaching for 16 years, was in charge of the inventory, police said. The thefts came to light when a student-owned sax, taken from the band room, was recovered at a pawn shop, and police found records of

27 other instruments that had been pawned. Broughton is charged with 28 counts of felony theft. (AP, UPI) ...*A band director should know that the piper must eventually be paid.*

Homework: Wally Bain, a teacher specializing in drug and alcohol abuse education for schools in Leesburg, Fla., says that students were extremely well versed in beer commercials and how to buy the suds, even though they are underage. Bain says some students know more about Budweiser frogs than about figures of U.S. history. (UPI) ...*That's because U.S. historical figures aren't on TV 536 times per day.*

Water-Gate: The Dutch Consumers' Union reports that in checks on 31 restaurants around Holland, 11 actually served carbonated tap water when customers ordered mineral water. The water was "exactly the same as water from a tap in the cafe's toilet," the report said. (AP) ...*In other words, it tastes like real mineral water.*

Pulling for your Country: A 1,500-man tug-of-war in Taipei, Taiwan, to commemorate the end of Japanese occupation ended almost immediately when the rope snapped. The sudden jerk yanked the arms off of two men who had wrapped the rope around their arms to get a better grip. Both had their limbs reattached by doctors. City officials plan to sue one of the men, city employee Chen Ming-kuo, for "dereliction of duty". (Reuters) ...*Chen does seem to inordinately suffer the whims of stupid jerks.*

Lost His Job at Lotus Development Corp.

Wanted: Suitable Position for Disoriented Indian Maharaja

AFP headline

Survival of the Specious: When Darwin Coates, 21, shoved a .22 caliber handgun into the waistband of his pants, it accidentally went off and shot him in the groin. He went into his girlfriend's Pasadena, Md., apartment to call for help. While waiting for an ambulance, his friend Gregory Johnson, 32, took the gun and stuck it in his back pocket. It accidentally went off and shot him in the buttocks. Both men required medical treatment. Police were able to recover the gun without shooting themselves. (Anne Arundel [Md.] Sun) ... *The Lady Smith & Wesson: a gun designed by women, for women.*

Pardon the Ring: When a man burst into West Bloomfield Township, Mich., Supervisor Jeddy Hood's office and took her hostage, she did what he asked: she called the governor to say an irate taxpayer demanded to speak with him or she would be killed. Gov. Engler's aides sprang into action, alerting the state police, which began "the process of implementing procedures." Luckily, one of those procedures was to notify the local police. Once they did, thirty minutes later, they found out what was really going on: a training exercise. Hood says she probably should have called someone else during the simulation, not the real governor. (AP) *...Don't call us, we'll call you.*

Game Time: The football team from the Laguna-Acoma (N.M.) High School was set to compete in the state playoffs, but the football season just stretched just a little too long — into hunting season. Five of the players quit the team so they wouldn't miss deer season. "It was a very easy decision," said the team's leading rusher, Kalvin Roughsurface. "Hunting is fun." Roughsurface and his brother Derrick, a tailback who is also quitting the team to hunt, note that one deer provides their family enough meat to last a year. (Lubbock [Texas] Avalanche-Journal) *...Not a difficult decision: one blood sport is pretty much like the next.*

A-Hunting We Will Go II: Michael Varriano, running for city council in Dilworth City, Minn., was declared the winner by one vote. But a mistake by election judges led to a recount: Varriano was told later in the week he actually lost by five votes. "Mike took it very well, he really did," said City Administrator Ken Parke. "He said he was going to go deer hunting and think about whether to ask for another recount." (Reuters) *...This is how movies of the week take root. Hollywood producers picture the opponent ending up shot to death in a "hunting accident" and....*

Softwear: British supermarket chain ASDA knew there might be trouble, but they did it anyway. "We released a range of knickers, bras and foundation-wear called 'microsoft'," an ASDA spokesman confirms, despite knowing that software giant Microsoft might object. However, "we didn't think there would be any confusion." The Seattle company did raise their legal hand, but have agreed to let the new label stand so long as ASDA doesn't capitalize the 'M' in microsoft. (Newsbytes) ... *"Thank you for calling technical support. For operating system questions, press 1; for applications, press 2; if your bra has failed causing your chest to crash, press 3...."*

Global Warning: New Zealand Environment Minister Simon Upton says the country should work to breed sheep and cows that do not burp as much. He says that the animals' belches, which have a high concentration of methane gas, add to the "greenhouse effect" which may lead to global warming. "As a proportion of our greenhouse gas emissions, our methane emissions are second to none," Upton says. New Zealand's sheep population is about 15 times larger than its human population. (AFP) ... *We like sheep who say baaaaa, not braaaaap.*

Coke Is It: McDonald's has opened its first restaurant in Bolivia. In addition to the usual menu of hamburgers and french fries, the high-altitude restaurant also serves items of more local interest, including tea made from coca leaves, the same kind used to make cocaine. (AP) ... *Sure the prices are high, but no one seems to care.*

Lettuce Pray: After a paper-mâché statue of the Virgin Mary at the Saint Peter and Paul church in Sannicola, Italy, began "crying tears", some said it was a miracle. But chemical analysis shows a more Earthly origin. The tears are a "substance like vegetable oil, very similar to olive oil," announced Bishop Vittorio Fusco, who collected the sample personally. (AFP) ... *It's a miracle! She's hungry!*

Clean Up This Town: David Snyder, 37, dropped his laundry off at his Vero Beach, Fla., cleaning service. But the employee who opened the bag found 3 pounds of marijuana inside, not dirty clothing. Police got a warrant to search Snyder's house, and found

$80,000 worth of pot plants, 8 pounds of processed marijuana, and an "elaborate" setup for growing the plants indoors. Snyder was arrested and charged with cultivation of marijuana, possession of more than 20 grams of marijuana, possession of drug paraphernalia and possession of marijuana with the intent to sell. (AP) *...You know how dumb the average person is? By definition, half the population is dumber than that.*

How Can You Tell When They're Not Wearing any Clothes?
Boys Will Be Boys —
But Never in the Nude
Reuters headline

No Such Thing as a Free Launch: A Seattle company says they have taken $5,000 deposits from 15 people for the company's "space experience" ride. Zegrahm Expeditions says they plan to launch six passengers at a time twice a week for three-hour suborbital spaceflights starting in 2001. The total cost per person will be $98,000. (AP) *...Even if they never launch, those people have already been taken on quite a ride.*

Space Cadets II: Employees of the London advertising agency The Mighty Big Idea "were sitting in the office and thinking, 'Where would be an amazing place to put adverts?'," says Gary Betts. They came up with the idea of launching mirrors into orbit that would project corporate logos on the moon. "The actual process is dangerously simple," Betts says. "It would be brilliant for a futuristic company." (Reuters) *...So everyone in the world could be totally sick of the "Golden Arches"? I don't think so.*

Demographic Party: While 89 percent of Chinese households now have a television set, only 2 percent have hot running water, according to a new national poll conducted by Gallup. Coca-Cola is the best-known foreign brand in China, with an 81 percent recognition rate. Per capita income has increased 75 percent since the last poll in 1994, perhaps reflecting the number-one "basic philosophy in life," which 56 percent said was "work hard and get rich." In the larger cities, nearly 75 percent of the women wear lipstick, but only 46 percent of city-dwellers even knew what socks are; nationwide, the sock recognition ratio is just 15 percent. (AP) *...That's Nike's fault. If they can't employ more than 15 percent of the Chinese population, they'll never be the Microsoft of softwear.*

Insert Tab 'A' into Slot 'B', Repeat as Necessary: Doctors in Singapore have solved part of the country's problem with infertility: they have found many couples don't know how to have sex, and have not been able to consummate their marriages "for years". "When a couple does not know how to engage in sexual intercourse, it results in infertility," says Dr. Ganesan Adaikan of the Society for the Study of Andrology and Sexology. (Reuters) *...Of course, they're the very people the state doesn't want reproducing in the first place.*

Medical Miracles II: Doctors in Thailand have solved part of the country's problem with the economy: they need to do more sex change operations. "Thailand has become the most popular place for sex change operations," Dr. Nikorn Dusitsil of the Institute of Medical Science Research told attendees at a Bangkok seminar. "Many foreigners are coming here to have the surgery and I think the income from this area will be able to help shore up the economy to a certain extent." A study reported at the seminar estimates that one man in 30,000 and one woman in 100,000 would like to switch gender. (Reuters) *...Which will lead to a horrifying imbalance in the spare parts market.*

Catisthenics: San Rafael, Calif., exercise enthusiast Stephanie Jackson says she has come up with a new piece of exercise equipment: a cat. Her new book, "Catflexing", describes "23 exercises which you and your cat can perform with every muscle group." Jackson said she got the tabby tone-up idea during a workout. "I was doing my bicep curls and my cat wanted to be held," she says. "I picked her up and started to pump her up and down, and the more I pumped, the more she purred." (AP) *...Yeah, like that video isn't produced 200 times a month in California already.*

Down the Up Staircase: St. Louis (Mo.) Fire Department rescuers released a man trapped in a chimney who, police think, may have been intent on burglarizing the warehouse at the bottom. However, "the chimney leads to a locked compressor room and he would have been locked in, anyway," a fire department spokesman said. "We've got a saying here in the fire department that goes, 'you can't fix stupid'." (UPI) ...*You could have if you had left him in the chimney.*

Office Accessory: Since 1911, every Rolls Royce has had a hood ornament called "The Spirit of Ecstasy". The Baron Montagu of Beaulieu has now revealed the model for the ornament. It was commissioned by his father, the 2nd Baron Montagu, who was editor of *The Car* magazine and the owner of a 1907 Rolls Silver Ghost. "The model... was my father's secretary, Eleanor Thornton," the current Baron says. "Actually," he adds, "she was a little more than a secretary." (AP) ...*In 1907, that's a reverent tribute. In 1997, it's a sexual harassment lawsuit.*

In His Image, Which Art Obscene: A exhibit of Rodin sculptures has been censored at Brigham Young University. The Mormon church-run school removed "Saint John The Baptist Preaching" because the nude depictions of the prophet, as well as "The Kiss", "The Prodigal Son" and "Monument to Balzac", "are such that the viewer will be concentrating on them in a way that is not good for us," said BYU Museum of Art's Director Campbell Gray. Gray rejected interpretations that the statue of Paul simply showed his mortality. "Everyone knows the prophet is mortal," he said. "But this conception... doesn't show the prophet side of the man at all." (AP) ...*Right, just his front and back.*

Up, Up and Away: Pilot Paul Sirks was out flying his vintage 1946 Aeronca Champ when he had mechanical problems and decided to land. After getting safely to the ground in Urbana, Ohio, the engine stalled on the runway. Needing to get it out of the way, he hopped out to restart it — he had to do it by turning the propellor by hand. That's when the engine started and the plane headed down the runway, Sirks running behind. "It just got away from him, and it took off," said an airport spokeswoman. "This plane also was trimmed for landing, which means the nose was trimmed up, so it just started climbing." With a plane from the state highway patrol in pursuit, the plane eventually reached 12,000 feet before it ran out of fuel and crashed 90 miles away. (AP) *...Any takeoff the pilot can walk away from is a bad one.*

But We Mean it in a Nice Way: The Federation of French Butchers is tired of news reports of murders using the words "butcher" and "butchery" to describe the crimes. The federation says the "butcher's role evokes peace and fraternity. There is nothing of the executioner or torturer about him." Rather than "butcher", the federation suggests news writers use words like "barbaric" instead. (UPI) *...What, and rile the Federation of French Barbers?*

You're In a Heap of Trouble, Boy

Researchers Can See Thoughts

UPI headline

War Games: During military training exercises, a consultant to the Israeli army yelled, "Western flank! Are you insane? What about the shrubbery?" The man, a civilian, was monitoring the damage tanks were doing to the plants in the desert training area. "This completely changes the planned attack," complained the general in charge of the games when told the vegetation's death toll was too high. But, he conceded, "just because we live under the threat of war does not mean everything else has to go on hold. When our peaceful future comes, we'll be happy we remembered the environment." (AP) *...Either that, or at least the cockroaches will have some ground cover after W.W.III.*

Dr. Seuss, M.D.: The U.S. government has drafted Dr. Seuss to help kids get immunized. A series of posters shows Seuss characters captioned with rhymes such as, "What's going on here? What's wrong with this fella? Why isn't he protected against measles, mumps and rubella?" The Centers for Disease Control and Prevention says 22 percent of 2-year-olds in the U.S. are not fully immunized. (AP) *...Works for older kids, too. "Don't run* *off, you come right back. You need a shot, yes sir, you do. You're stuck, you're stuck in a nasty trap. Roll up your sleeve, you've got the clap."*

Texas Truck Tales: Benny Patterson II, 27, and Lynn Morse, 41, enjoyed playing "chicken". Whenever one would see the other on the highway, they would aim at each other and see which man would swerve away first. Recently spotting each other on a farm road north of Waco, Texas, they finally met, head-on, each going about 60 mph. Patterson, wearing a seatbelt in his airbag-equipped pickup, survived the wreck. Morse, not wearing a seatbelt in his pickup, was killed. Patterson spent the next day trying to explain the joke to Morse's two children, aged 7 and 9. (Houston Chronicle) ... *"'I was only kidding' is the social equivalent of the insanity defense." —Judith "Miss Manners" Martin.*

Candy, Little Boy? A Colorado Springs, Colo., school district says it did the right thing when it suspended 6-year-old Seamus Morris under the school's zero-tolerance drug policy. The drug? Lemon drops. Taylor Elementary School administrators called an ambulance after a teacher saw the boy give another student some candy, which was a brand teachers didn't recognize. "It was not something you would purchase in a grocery store," a district spokesman said. "It was from a health-food store." A spokesman for St. Claire's Lemon Tarts, however, noted that the candy is indeed sold in Colorado's largest grocery store chain. School officials were not impressed, and not only upheld the half-day suspension, but told the boy's mother that a child who brings candy to school is comparable to a teen who takes a gun to school. (UPI) ...*Maybe it's time for a "zero-tolerance policy" toward idiotic school administrators.*

Candy, Little Boy? II: A 10-year-old girl at McElwain Elementary in Thornton, Colo., was one of a group of girls who "repeatedly" asked a certain boy on the playground if he liked them. The boy complained to a teacher, so school administrators, citing the district's "zero-tolerance sexual harassment policy", decided to suspend her. After an outcry from outraged parents, the school changed its mind. A district spokeswoman said school officials "probably" overreacted, but "it's all in how you look at it." (UPI) *...Same apple, different worms.*

Recess: An 11-year-old Egyptian student showed up at the airport in Alexandria and asked for a ticket to Canada, where he planned to ask for asylum from his schoolteachers. Airport ticket agents called his mother instead of accepting the $800 cash he offered for the ticket. Meanwhile, 16-year-old Fenn Chapman, who had disappeared from his boarding school in Britain, was found taking a "stress break" from exams on the beaches of Barbados. Fellow students took up a collection to buy him the plane ticket. "All the lads knew about his idea but a lot thought he would never really do it," a fellow student said. (AFP, 2) *...Oh, does "I dare yuh" still work on school kids?*

Undercover: The Infectious Diseases Research Center at Canada's Laval University in Quebec City says it has developed an "invisible condom". Laval hopes the condom, made of two liquids that solidify into a waterproof film when mixed and warmed to body temperature, will hit the market within two years. (Reuters) *...Really, babe! I'm wearing one!*

Go Topless, Save Your Life: The Northern California Cancer Center says exposure to sunlight could lower the risk of breast cancer in women by 30–40 percent, and maybe more. "It is possible that all it takes is 10 or 15 minutes outside in bright sunlight to get a benefit," said NCCC epidemiologist Esther John. "But we don't really know that yet. There needs to be more study." But, she warns, too much sun could lead to skin cancer trouble. "We know now that a little bit of sun is beneficial, but it is not good to stay out there four or five hours. We don't want to recommend that people go out and bake in the sun." (AP) *...Remember: tan lines can kill.*

Beats Me: The California Supreme Court has ruled that feet are not deadly weapons. The case involved Raymond Aguilar; in his trial for aggravated assault, the prosecutor told the jury that Aguilar's hands and feet were "deadly weapons". The court said no, under California law, a deadly weapon must be "an object extrinsic to the body." (Reuters) ...*Such as, say, really bad foot odor.*

Parts is Parts: John Bisius, of Bulawayo, Zimbabwe, lost both of his legs in a mining accident 16 years ago. He's now decided he wants them back. "If my bones were buried I want to dig them up. I will keep them and wait for my other part to die so that I can be buried in one grave," he said. "If it was just a finger, I would probably not complain. I have never heard of a person being buried in two graves." (AFP) ...*Never heard of land mines, John?*

Be Careful What You Ask For

"It's me or the iguana," she said. "The iguana," he replied.
AFP headline

Take One Down and Pass it Around: Police in Johannesburg, South Africa, arrested a man who had arrived on a flight from Sao Paolo, Brazil, as a suspected drug courier. "There was hardly place for a biscuit in the man's stomach," a police spokesman said, because he had swallowed 99 cocaine-filled condoms to smuggle them into the country. "A few years back we had a guy who had swallowed 90. This is a record," the spokesman added. "To the great relief of himself and the detectives, the suspect passed the last of [them] last night." (Reuters) ...*It's "99 Bottles of Beer on the Wall" updated for the 90s.*

Stinky Excuse: When Peter Chiafos, Jr., was arrested in Cedar Rapids, Iowa, he had an explanation. Charged with sexual misconduct for fondling a 6-year-old boy and a 7-year-old girl, Chiafos told police he was "not himself" and had possibly been "overcome" by air freshener he had sprayed in his truck. Judge William Thomas was not impressed by the explanation: he sentenced Chiafos to 10 years in prison. (Cedar Rapids Gazette) ...*Don't worry, Pete: your fellow inmates in the showers aren't themselves. They were overcome by the steam. Feel better?*

Mutton, Honey: Police in Hamurana, New Zealand, stopped a car because its passengers were acting "suspiciously". Once the officer approached the car, he noticed one of the passengers "appeared to be cuddling a large woolly object." A live sheep. Three more were baaing from the trunk. The passengers, four men aged 17, 24, 27 and 32, were charged with the theft of the four animals. (New Zealand Herald) ...*So much for their plans to practice animal husbandry.*

Clergy Clarification: The Vatican has issued a proclamation to clarify the roles of the laity in the Catholic church. Due to a shortage of priests, lay helpers have been taking an increasingly larger role in church functions, even assisting in weddings, funerals, and Sunday services. But never, the church says, in celebrating Mass, which must be done by a priest. (AP) ...*In summary, priests do more than lay people.*

Vatican II: The Vatican's newspaper, Osservatore Romano, quoted "staunch moralist theologian" Father Gino Concetti as saying, "Homosexuals do have the right to be considered to be different, to practice their homosexuality, to live together, to make up a couple and to have children. They do have the right to adopt children and even to demand social rights." An angry Concetti sought an explanation: he said that wasn't what he wrote for the paper. Editor Gianfranco Grieco claims a computer virus removed several "nots" from the article. "These things do happen," he claimed. (AFP) ...*Now that **is** news: The Vatican has a shortage of "nots"!*

Who's that Tapping on My Door? Kia Motors admits there is a strange defect in the 1997 Sportage sport utility vehicle. Tapping the car in the right spot will disengage its security system and unlock the doors. Kia says they will not issue a recall of the vehicle since the problem is not a "safety issue". (UPI) ...*In other words, Kia is pretty sure no one would ever want to steal one.*

Fall Down, Go Boom: Pacific Gas & Electric Company says sorry, it looks like that was their fault. Dawn Mabalon says she parked her Toyota over a manhole in San Francisco. Under the street, PG&E says they had accidentally hooked up a new natural gas pipe to an old, leaky pipe. Seeping gas flooded the utility space, then came up through the manhole and into Mabalon's engine compartment. When she turned the key to start the engine, the gas — and her car — exploded. Mablon and her passenger were slightly injured. "I'll never park on that side of the street again," she said. (UPI) ...*Right. Next time, for safety, park in front of the Greasy Chili Diner.*

D) All of the Above: A survey by "Who's Who Among American High School Students" finds that 76 percent "of the brightest U.S. high school students" have cheated in school, either by copying someone else's homework or by cheating on exams. (Reuters) *...How do they know, then, these are bright students? Maybe they cheated on that test, too.*

Solidarity: Romanian soothsayers have had it with "imposters" taking customers away from them. "Many people who have got nothing to do with this business are pretending to be able to tell the future and stealing our clients," one clairvoyant complained. Their solution: unionization. "Only those who can prove their ability to tell the future and lift evil spells from people will be admitted to our union." (AFP) *...Go figure: a union that no one will ever be allowed to join.*

Absolutely Positive: Wendy Cannon has finished her study at Canada's Vancouver General Hospital. She followed the progress of several people who were attacked by grizzly bears, which typically weigh 300 to 800 pounds. The victims had torn-off scalps, serious lacerations, and other injuries. Each needed 31 to 55 days of hospital care after their life-threatening attacks. Her conclusion: grizzly bear attacks lead to nightmares and psychological problems such as post-traumatic stress disorder. (UPI) *...Cannon's next study: finding out whether researchers like it when you give them million-dollar study grants.*

Gastronomically Correct
Caribbean Bananas Are Ethical Bananas —UK Minister
Reuters headline
British MPs to Drink Ethically Produced Coffee
Another Reuters headline from the same day

Der Cataloguefüror: When catalog merchant Lands' End offered German customers the same thing it offers customers in 175 other countries — a lifetime warranty on their clothing — an organization of German retailers sued them for "unfair competition". The merchants lost. "Trying to make a customer completely happy is still a very new concept here," said the head of the company's German subsidiary. (Newsweek) *...Shirts not stiff enough? We'll take 'em back! Sweaters not scratchy enough? We'll take 'em back! Boots don't cause blisters? We'll take 'em back!*

For Richer, For Milk Money: Some parents in Dover, Del., are upset that their second-grade children were "married" to each other by their teacher. The classroom event at Star Hill Elementary paired same-sex students together to pledge their friendship, to share, and to play nice. One parent said the lesson "condoned homosexuality" and vowed to take her son out of the school. Teacher Ede Outten said it was little different than children singing "I love you, you love me" on the "Barney" TV show. "Even Barney's intentions would be suspect in Dover," she said. (AP) *...And rightly so.*

Veni, Vidi, Tipsi: The Michelin man, the corporate spokes-cartoon for the French tire company, is being updated for the millennium with a slimmer look. The character, which debuted in 1898, looks like a stack of white tires with a face and arms. His name is Bibendum, after a line in a Latin verse of Horace which appeared with a beer-chugging Bibendum in 1898, "Nunc est bibendum," which roughly translates to "Now is the time to drink." (Reuters)

...That slogan will also be updated for the millennium, to "If you drink, don't drive. If you must drink and drive, ride on Michelins."

Tamagotcha: Wanting in on some of the action that rival Bandai is getting with their Tamagotchi ("cute little egg") virtual pet toy, Japan's Takara Co. Ltd. is bringing out Neko Unjatta ("I produced a cat"), which allows players to "mate" their electronic pets together to breed offspring. By using the "love-love communication function", two toys ("You have to be careful, because you cannot 'communicate' two males together or two females together," Takara says) can produce kittens which can themselves mate after a week of growth. Cute? Think again: an eight-month-old Yorkshire Terrier was turned in to a London animal shelter in favor of a Tamagotchi. A shelter spokesman said two children dumped their pet, and their father "was very shamefaced when he explained that his children loved their computer pets more than a real dog" after they found the dog "needs a lot of attention." (AFP, 2) *...He should have dropped off the kids instead.*

Like Father, Like Son: Bill Wells had not seen his son since the boy was 2 months old, 22 years before. He didn't think he'd see him anytime soon, either, since Wells was locked up in the Kerr County (Texas) Jail on a burglary charge. But when Corey Hillger was jailed in Kerr County on a burglary charge of his own, Wells quickly recognized the kid. The father and son reunion led to hugs and a lot of catching up. "It's a God deal. It was a miracle," Wells said. "I was ecstatic. I never heard of anything like a father and son meeting in jail," Hillger agreed. (AP) *...Just a chip off the old cell block.*

Daddy Dearest: A man in Kinshasa, Democratic Republic of Congo, was upset to learn that three of his four children were not his own, and that his wife of 20 years had been unfaithful to him for most of that time. Worse, the neighbors had known for a long time and laughed at him behind his back. Furious, "Papa G." sent the wife and three girls to the kids' father's house to live, but then decided that wasn't revenge enough. So he seduced one of the girls, got her pregnant, and married her to become his ex-wife's son-in-law. (AFP) *...Kinshasa: in the U.S., we pronounce that "Kennedy".*

The Shape of Things to Come: Barbie dolls are being updated for a "more youthful and more contemporary" look, Mattel has announced. Less makeup, smaller breasts, a thicker waist, and slimmer hips are all slated for the new look. The doll's original shape, which if expanded to adult size would produce measurements of 38-18-34, has long been criticized. Feminists say Barbie's shape is "unrealistic and creates the wrong ideal for young girls" who may "aspire to a body type they can never achieve." (AP) ...*Why didn't they criticize the Cabbage Patch dolls for the same reason?*

Show and Tell: Britain's first "Erotica Exhibition" was a success. People queued around the block to get in to see the "Fetishist Village", condom stands, body piercing, chocolate-flavored body paint, and all the usual toys and gadgets. "Sex is fun. That is our message," said organizer Brian Wiseman. "Throw off your inhibitions. Come. Laugh. Enjoy and Smile." (Reuters) ...*Though not necessarily in that order.*

Show and Tell II: Brazil's first "Erotika Fair" didn't do too well. Sao Pauloans mostly yawned over the kinky exhibits. Some things were popular, such as glow-in-the-dark condoms, considered a good "Christmas stocking stuffer". The hit attraction: a "Libido Tour" where topless tour guides escorted visitors through a tunnel where strangers would pop out of the shadows to fondle passers-by. "This was the best thing here. There were real men in the tunnel," said one enthusiastic woman. All in all, however, the fairgoers seemed bored. Sales of "erotica staples," including videos, are low in the country, with per capita spending at only about $3 per year, far below American and European levels, and attendance at the fair was less than half of the 50,000 expected. (Reuters) ...*That's OK: the Newcastle coal show didn't do well either.*

What I Really Want to Do is Direct: A 36-year-old New Zealand man has pled guilty to nine counts of illegal "shu-cam" operations. The man used a tiny shoe-mounted camera to record the view up the skirts of "thousands" of women and girls at public events. Caught after boasting of his exploits on the Internet, he was not charged for assault, sexual exploitation, or invasion of privacy. He was charged under New Zealand's Films, Videos and Publications Act. (Reuters) ...*Everyone wants to be a critic.*

But a Lot of Ambassadors Had to be Paid Off to Get it Done

29 Nations Approve Bribery Ban
AP headline

'Tis the Season: "Father Christmas is unfortunately unable to reply to the children's letters he receives at this time of the year," announced the Santa Claus of Greenland Foundation. "But Santa loves hearing from children and wants them to continue writing to him." The foundation has stopped their earlier practice of sending presents to the children who write, but they still like getting the letters because they sell the stamps from the envelopes to collectors. However, they'll make an exception to the gift-giving: if children write on a special postcard, which can be bought for 20 crowns, they'll reply with a gift "From Santa". (Reuters) ...*It's so nice that Christmas (registered trademark, all rights reserved) isn't as commercial as it once was.*

'Tis the Season II: This is make or break time for the 14 monks at Assumption Abbey in Ava, Mo. This year, they turned out 23,000 fruitcakes in 10 months from the monastery's bakery for last-minute shipment all over the world for Christmas. The monastery has been making fruitcakes for 10 years, after failing to make enough money from their previous avocation, making concrete blocks. (AP) ...*At least they were able to use the same recipe and molds.*

'Tis the Season III: Police in Leeds, England, are hand-delivering Christmas greetings to dozens of people. Not just anyone, actually: only known thieves. The front of the special card reads "Season's Greetings". Inside, the legend reads, "Police will be actively targeting known burglars this Christmas." Officers hope the message will be clear. A police spokesman said "It is a case of just knocking on the door, saying do not do it again, [and putting] something in someone's hand to warn them." (AFP)

*...The bobbies are apparently the ones who **really** know who's naughty or nice.*

Naughty or Nice II: Victoria, B.C., Canada, shopping mall Santa Allan Turner met his match in a naughty little girl who kicked him in the groin and pulled his beard down to his waist. In response, he wouldn't give her a candy cane. Mall management was unsympathetic: they fired him. He was relieved, then, when another Victoria-area mall hired him to play Santa. With reporters covering his first day at work, Turner turned to a local TV station's camera and said, "I suppose you want a picture of me protecting my jangles." The former soccer coach then grabbed his crotch, imitating, he said later, "a grip used by athletes to protect their 'penalty zones'." The image was broadcast on the evening news. Mall management was unsympathetic: they fired him. Turner tearfully told reporters he doesn't know what he's going to do now. He said the stunt "was a bad judgment call," but "can't you make a joke anymore?" (Victoria Times Colonist) *...As a former coach, Santa should have known how important it is to wear your "cup of cheer" at all times.*

Store Santa II: Irish member of parliament Michael Moynihan is urging stores to set some standards for the Santa Claus actors they hire this year. He wants them to ban "crusty" types and "dupes in tacky beards and scruffy red suits who can't give a decent Ho, Ho, Ho." He says such poor role models devalue the spirit of Christmas. (Reuters) *...Sounds fair. They'll do it the moment Parliament sets some standards for politicians.*

Just in Time for Christmas: An entrepreneur in Phnom Penh, Cambodia, is opening a new attraction on Christmas Eve. It's a shooting range, with fully automatic weapons. "It's every little boy's dream to play with guns," said Victor Chao. "Shooting an automatic weapon is like having a multiple orgasm." But that's not all. Visitors will also be able to launch grenades and B-40 rockets on the 48-lane firing range. "We wanted to create another tourist attraction in Cambodia besides Tuol Sleng and the Killing Fields," Chao said. "We wanted to create something a bit more entertaining." He has named the attraction "War Disney". (AFP)

...After having rejected "Mother Goose's Explodatorium" and "The Dr. Seuss Gatling Gunnery".

Just in Time II: Northwestern Mutual Insurance Co. has issued a report saying that Santa's activities would put him in a high risk insurance classification. While they consider him an "experienced pilot," his landing on icy rooftops increases his risk. His life insurance rates would be higher than average because of his pipe smoking and "bowl of jelly" belly. Worse, "life insurance rates are based on the age of the insured. And Santa Claus is, after all, ageless," the Milwaukee, Wisc., company says. The reindeer would have to be insured against damaging roofs of the visited houses, and "special event" coverage would be a good idea in case any presents fall out of the sleigh as it flies overhead. (UPI) *...So much added cost this year! First, GPS navigation and radar collision avoidance systems, and now this!*

True Meaning of Christmas: Lingerie maker Victoria's Secret is hoping to sell a special, one of a kind gift item this Christmas: a $3 million strapless bra with 99 diamonds along the top seam and a 42-carat rock dangling in the cleavage. "No one seems really serious about buying it, though people are interested in the stones," a spokeswoman said, adding "it's not really a bra, it's a wonderful holiday top you would wear under a jacket where you can see the center." (Reuters) *...Typical: everyone admires the wrapping but forgets about the lovely presents inside.*

And Here You Were Afraid We Wouldn't Give You Anything This Year

U.S. Workers Getting Pink Slips for Christmas
Reuters headline

Make a Getaway in Your Chevrolet: Heather Beckwith, 18; Curtis Johnson, 19; Michael Guilbault, 19; and Justin Lowery, 17, were driving around Raleigh, N.C., looking for just the right place to rob, prosecutors say. Once they chose a spot, Beckwith and Johnson hid the car in a dark spot while Guilbault and Lowery went into the store. When they came out, they found Beckwith and Johnson in the getaway car, in the dark, with the doors locked, "steaming up the windows," Assistant DA Jeffrey Cruden said. They told Guilbault and Lowery to "be patient." Once the couple "completed the act" they unlocked the doors. By then, witnesses had a good description of the car and the four were arrested. Johnson and Lowery have been charged with robbery and await trial, Guilbault has pleaded guilty to robbery, and Beckwith has pleaded guilty to being an accessory after the fact. (Raleigh News and Observer) ...*That's not what I meant when I said "Let's hit the Quickie Mart."*

Photo Op: When Lynn Wilkinson of Jacksonville Beach, Fla., and her son Andy, 9, visited Alltel Stadium, one thing they saw was a 16-foot bronze statue of the Jacksonville Jaguars' mascot. Wilkinson told Andy to stick his head in the statue's mouth for a photo. After mom got the snap, Andy found he was stuck. It took rescuers an hour to cut through one of the statue's fangs to release the boy, to the applause of a crowd that had gathered. (AP) ...*Just in time to leave for their next photo stop, the zoo.*

Mistaken Identity: Police in Bangkok, Thailand, arrested an American tourist who climbed repair scaffolding to the top of Wat Arun (Temple of the Dawn) and refused to come down. After 10 hours, the man was subdued by police and turned over to the American Embassy. He identified himself as God, but officials determined he was Brandon Simcock, 27, an employee of Microsoft. (Bangkok Post) ... *"Termination Notice. Reason for Termination: Impersonating CEO."*

Walk This Way: Peoria, Ill., police think Christina Mack, 35, intended to kill her one-legged boyfriend after they had an argument over her 6-week pregnancy. Mack allegedly used household oil to grease up the floor at the top of the stairs so that her boyfriend, Chester Parkman, 50, would slip and fall. The scheme came to light when firefighters were called to the house to render first aid after Mack slipped on the oil and fell, knocking her unconscious. Parkman first told police Mack had tried to kill him, but later told a local newspaper, "I honestly think she was trying to wax the floor." Police charged her with domestic battery, rather than attempted murder. (AP) *...When partner perpetrates improper punishment and police promise prosecution, pegleg Parkman punts to prevent pregnant prole's presentation to Peoria penitentiary.*

Don't Worry, Be Happy: A Louis Harris Research survey shows that most women think they are happier than their mothers were at the same age. The survey, conducted in the U.S., Britain, France, Italy, Germany and Spain, found that the number one reason women cited for the happiness boost is the increased availability of contraception since their mothers' time. (Reuters) *...Translation: "I think my mother would have been happier if she could have prevented my birth."*

Have It Your Way: Prison guards transporting 11 inmates from Kansas to Florida stopped at a Burger King in Owatonna, Minn., for lunch. When one guard went in to order, the prisoners tossed the other guard out the van's door and took off. When the van was found later, eight were still inside; two others were caught within 20 minutes. Meanwhile, two guards employed by a private security firm transporting prisoners from Memphis, Tenn., to Georgia have been arrested after allegedly drinking during the trip. Police say the two guards got into a fight, and the driver stopped and pushed the other guard out the door and drove off. The driving guard was charged with drunk driving; the guard who was pushed out was charged with filing a false police report after he told officers that the prisoners had pushed him out and had taken the driver hostage. And both were charged with sharing their booze with the prisoners. The prisoners were not charged with any crime. "They didn't do anything wrong," said a county sheriff. "They were given a beverage and they partook." (AP, 2) *...And for just 39 cents, they could have Supersized it.*

Inmate Alcohol II: Cosmo Zinkow, an eighth grader at Griffin Middle School in Atlanta, Ga., gave his teacher a special gift for Christmas: a bottle of Mouton Cadet Bordeaux. The teacher, following school policy, told the principal about the gift. The principal, following district policy, suspended Zinkow for 10 days for possessing alcohol on campus. Zinkow's father is furious. "When you take a Christmas gift to the teacher, wrapped and in a box with a bow and a card, that's not possessing alcohol," he said. "I felt like this was an appropriate gift for her." (Reuters) *...If it were the 1994 vintage, and not that off-year swill he got, sure.*

Also Available in Cantaloupe: French lingerie manufacturer Neyret has come out with a new line of "intelligent" underwear. The first product, a bra, is made from special fabric encapsulated with perfume so the garment can emit a scent when the bra is caressed. "We wanted to stimulate the nighttime market and this is what we came up with," a company spokesman said. Neyret says the bra's aroma is a combination of "pink grapefruit, apple, watermelon, blackcurrant and pink apricots." (Reuters) *...Watermelon and grapefruit, eh? What a surprise.*

Scapegoat of the Year

El Niño Blamed for Rise in Diarrhea in Peru
Reuters headline

Hurry, Sale Ends Tuesday: A police officer in Suffield, Conn., noticed a speeding car that matched the description of a robbery getaway car from nearby Agawam, Mass. He started pursuit. During the chase, the suspect "made a wrong turn" — into the MacDougall Correctional Institution, a high-security prison. He then jumped from his car and dashed into the lobby. "I believe he thought it was a mall," said officer Michael Lewandowski after capturing Vincent McKenzie, 32, and booking him on multiple charges. "But I've never seen too many malls with a razor wire across the top." (AP) *...Give them a few years.*

Career Counseling: A poll of Russian teenagers has found some interesting career ambitions. The poll, conducted on the Sakhalin Peninsula, found that 25 percent of the girls said they would like to become prostitutes and 27 percent of the boys said they want to be racketeers. Nine percent said they want to be contract killers.

(AP) ...They'll need that many to clear out the excessive numbers of racketeers.

Y'all Come Down Here, Hear? Houston, Texas, wanted to spruce up its image a bit and attract more visitors, so it inserted 4 million scratch-off, instant win game pieces in a magazine, giving away 33 free trips to the city. Only one of the prizes was claimed, and only 1,200 people registered for the "second chance" drawing. "Clearly, the message we've gotten back is that there weren't a lot of fish out there biting on the bait," grumbled City Councilman Rob Todd. (Reuters) *...First prize, a week in Houston. Second prize, two weeks in Houston.*

Blimey: An 11-year-old British schoolboy met an Australian class-mate and greeted him by saying, "G'day, sport." The boy, who was not named, was "caught" by a teacher, the school said in a statement, and while "there was no maliciousness or intent" on the boy's part, he was charged with racism for his greeting. "The boy was counseled, ...dialogue has taken place with parents," and the boy was made to write "I must not use racist remarks" 60 times, said the statement by Beverley Grammar School in York-shire. Tony Brett Young of the Australian High Commission was concerned it was a case of political correctness gone overboard. "'G'day sport' is part of our vernacular," he said. "It's just a traditional and friendly manner of speaking." (Reuters) *...Tony, you must remember that the self-appointed paternalistic PC snobs don't care what you think as they're more "culturally sensitive" of your nationality than you.*

Fourth Floor, Furs and Outerwear: Police in Vaesteraas, Swe-den, said they suspected it would be a wild goose chase when they got the call: a hotel said a doe and her two fawns were found in a second-floor ballroom. Police inspector Bengt Ottervald, a vet-eran hunter, was called in. He "talked gently" to the animals and helped them down the stairs and back outside. Meanwhile, crows reportedly chased a coyote through downtown Seattle. When it passed the Henry M. Jackson Federal Building, a sensor automat-ically opened the door. The coyote accepted the mechanical invitation and ran straight into an open elevator. "Fortunately there was no one in the elevator," a government spokesman said.

It took animal control officers nearly 3 hours to capture it and move it to a more rural area. (AFP, AP) ...*Most of that time was spent in intense questioning about the "fertilizer" it left in the building.*

Autoerotic: British doctors have reported they cured a woman of her orgasms. The unidentified woman, 44, "would suddenly become aware of an internal, ascending feeling indistinguishable from an orgasm," her doctors, Robert Will and Paul Reading of Edinburgh's Western General Hospital, wrote in the medical journal Lancet, noting it cropped up without warning, sometimes while driving, which she thought was dangerous. "Owing to their nature," they said, such problems "may [be reported] to physicians late." Indeed, she only complained when one episode left her unconscious. A brain scan found a minor abnormality. She was put on an epileptic drug, which has stopped the orgasms. (Reuters) ...*Lucky for her: the usual way to stop orgasms is to get married.*

More More More: A study by researchers from Belfast and Bristol universities has found that sexually active men live longer. "Mortality risk was 50 percent lower in the group with high orgasmic frequency than in the group with low orgasmic frequency," the researchers, led by Dr. George Davey Smith, reported. "Sexual activity seems to have a protective effect on men's health." The men, aged 45–49, were studied over a decade. Their sexual activity was classified on a scale from "never" to "daily". The British Medical Journal was quick to note that the study could be used as the basis for new "healthy living" advertising campaigns. "Intervention programmes could be considered, perhaps based on the exciting 'at least five a day' campaign aimed at increasing fruit and vegetable consumption — although the numerical imperative may have to be adjusted," it wrote in an editorial. (Reuters)... *"George will do just about anything to prove the point he tried to make when we got married," Mrs. Smith told newspapers.*

Michael Kennedy Fit
Kennedy Image

AP headline

Picture Perfect Politician: Mayor Craig S. Johnson, 41, of Snow Hill, Md., has been arrested for allowing a woman to pose naked on the top of a sheriff's squad car assigned to him. The mayor, who also worked as a deputy sheriff, allegedly contacted the operator of a pornographic Internet web site and offered to help do the photos as a "prank" since he was leaving the sheriff's department. The photos came to light when local high school students found the pictures on the web site. The mayor was charged with two counts of misdemeanor misconduct in office. (AP) *...He offered them his honor, they honored him his offer.*

Tall Tale: Author Erich Segal has quashed reports that Vice President Al Gore was the model for the male character in his 1970 best-seller, "Love Story". Gore told reporters he was the model for the book, written by fellow Harvard University student Segal. But Segal, reacting to the reports, says it's not true: Oliver Barrett IV was based on actor Tommy Lee Jones, who also went to Harvard. A Gore spokeswoman said Gore "never misspoke" in making the claim, but "he may have been misheard." (AFP) *...Right. Segal actually said Gore was the model for "Forrest Gump".*

Love Story II: An Egyptian businessman got jealous when he returned home and found his young, pretty wife was not there. Suspecting her of being unfaithful, when she returned he pronounced the "talaq", a triple renunciation which legally divorced her from him. Thinking better of it later, he ran up against a problem: under Moslem law, a husband cannot remarry his wife until she has first married someone else, then divorced again, so he paid one of his employees to marry her for one day. Now he has another problem: the next morning, the employee refused to divorce her. The impatient wife has now filed for divorce so she can return to her wealthy first husband. (AFP) ...*Now there's a story we could believe happened to Al Gore.*

Dead Man Walking: Daniel Earl Bales Jr. will soon leave a Colorado prison. Then he'll start working on solving his next problem: "I'm dead," he says, "and I'm really concerned about that." In 1987, Bales escaped from prison and managed to stay on the lam for nine years. In 1991, after hearing nothing from him, his wife petitioned for a death certificate so she could collect on a life insurance policy. Now, Bales has to figure out how to get a driver's license and a Social Security card so he can get a job. "We honestly believed he was dead. We went through all sorts of efforts to locate him," said Marshall Quiat, the wife's lawyer. "The statute was followed completely, and done in good faith. If the poor son of a bitch is dead, that's his problem." (Denver Post) ...*"I think, therefore I am" is a philosophical paradigm, not a guarantee from government bureaucrats.*

So Help Me Gods: A Minneapolis, Minn., judge has turned down a motion filed in a lawsuit to allow a curse to be performed in his courtroom. The "native" ceremony, meant to cause the death of any person in the case who lied to the court, would have been performed by the plaintiff, a Hmong woman. Judge Harry Crump complained, "I cannot believe you are seriously making a motion like that to this court. Court rules of decorum do not allow demonstrations within the courtroom area," he said, adding, "I'm sure the gods will understand." (AP) ...*They probably already know that perjury is not a capital offense in the U.S.*

Jaws: A Russian fisherman was taken to the hospital to get a fish that he caught removed — from his face. The man held up the bumper pike for his friends to see when it bit his nose. Despite hacking the body off, the fish still wouldn't let go. Doctors had to pry the disembodied jaws loose. (Reuters) ...*You should have seen the fisherman who got away!*

Takes One to Know One: Police in Lee's Summit, Mo., arrested a security guard for indecent exposure when they found him running down the street naked. Gary Aicard, 51, a guard at an office building, told officers he had stripped because he thought it would help him find "the real streaker" since their mutual nudity would help him make friends with him. Police didn't buy the story. Meanwhile, a British tourist got naked and jumped over the boards at a hockey game in Calgary, Alberta, Canada, and ran around on the ice for several minutes before police and security arrived to escort him to jail. The stunt, before 17,000 fans, interrupted the game between the Calgary Flames and the Florida Panthers at the Saddledome. (AP, 2) ...*It's sad to see people who can't keep violence and sex separate.*

Don't Worry Your Pretty Little Head Over It: Worrying about your weight makes you stupid. Or, at least, it impairs your memory. Britain's Institute of Food Research studied women who were on a diet and found they performed worse on memory tests than other women who merely were careful about what they ate. Researchers at the institute conclude that the results are due to the women using "too much brain capacity" to worry about their diets. "The kind of effect we are talking about is the preoc-cupation that you would find with somebody who is ...worried about taking a stressful exam," the study's author said. (Reuters) *...Or the kind of overload that results from upgrading to the new version of "Windows".*

Michael Jackson Turned Away at Border
Please Visit Cairo but Without Your Chimpanzee Friends, Officials Say
AFP headline

If There's No Beer, Why Go There? Despite a new Miller beer ad showing partying angels quaffing their brew, there's no beer in Heaven, insists Rev. Edward Smart of Newark, N.J. Saying the TV commercial is blasphemous, Smart says it is "theologically dangerous to assume that angels in Heaven ...are alcoholics." The Religiously Correct minister claims the spot "says that God sanctions beer, alcohol [and] substance abuse," but "God doesn't [sanction] that." Miller is unrepentant. "We have received a tremendous amount of positive feedback," a spokeswoman says. "People get that it's very lighthearted." (AP) *...Except for the people who think God has no sense of humor.*

Going to Hell in a Beer Truck II: The U.S. Second Circuit Court of Appeals has overruled the New York State Liquor Authority's decision to censor the picture of Bad Frog Brewery's mascot on its beer labels. "A picture of a frog with the second of its four unwebbed 'fingers' extended in a manner evocative of a well known human gesture of insult has presented this Court with significant issues concerning First Amendment protections for commercial speech," the court said. Jim Waldron, president of the Michigan brewery, is upset that his victory took so long. "This fight has been ridiculous from the beginning. Bad Frog and the taxpayers of New York have lost millions because these guys don't have a sense of humor," he said. "I thought the middle finger was the state bird in New York." (Reuters, UPI) *...Huh: I just thought the frog was proclaiming "We're Number One in Bad Taste".*

Full Service: A new British mall is building in an innovation to attract women shoppers: a day care center — for their husbands. "Some grown-up men are very similar to small children, and most couples have anecdotes of their own to prove it," said a spokesman for the Bluewater Retail Centre, being constructed in Kent. He added that the idea for the big-baby-sitting area came from "extensive research showing that 50 percent of couples' shopping trips end in argument." The creche features video games, televisions showing sports ...and beer. (Reuters) *...And, we hope, a changing area.*

You Know You're Having a Bad Day When: After police in Oxnard, Calif., pulled Kevin Wallace over for speeding, his 3-year-old son leaned out the car window to the officer. "Here," he said, holding out a bag of marijuana. "Bad," he informed the cop as he handed it over. Bad indeed: Wallace was arrested and charged with speeding, driving with a suspended license, driving under the influence of alcohol, not having his son in a child seat, possession of marijuana and child endangerment. But he isn't angry at his toddler. "I'm glad he did it," Wallace said. "It makes you want to stop using drugs." Why did the boy think the pot was bad? Wallace and his wife taught him that drugs were wrong. "We taught him well," Wallace said. (AP) *...Yes indeed, despite the "do as I say, not as I do" field work.*

Give 'em an Inch and They'll Take a Mile: When the female giraffe at the Abilene, Texas, zoo died, it left the remaining male giraffe lonely. So volunteers held a fund-raiser to collect $20,000 to purchase him a new mate, "selling inches" of the new giraffe for $5 and "selling spots" on it for $100. The fund-raising group sold 1,326 inches and 70 spots, bringing forth visions of an exceptionally spotty, 110-foot-tall animal, but a few people took "spots" rather generically: donors also "bought" the giraffe's ears, eyes, neck, and the back of its head. A local gynecologist won the most unusual portion: he got dibs on its reproductive system. (Lubbock Avalanche-Journal) *...Hey, pal, you bought it, so you have to do the maintenance on it.*

Prerequisite: Schools in Israel are planning a new course to help the country "shed its reputation for aggressive and noisy public behavior," the National Institute for Education and Democracy says. The class, to teach children how to wait patiently in line, is scheduled to begin in a month. (Reuters) *...What's taking so long? Do you know how long I've been waiting for this class? Do you think I've got nothing better to do than wait for you?*

His Face Rings a Bell: New York newspapers have dubbed a band of robbers "The Three Stooges" after a heist at the World Trade Center. The trio managed to bypass multiple checkpoints and security guards and escape with $1.17 million in cash, but they removed their masks before they got out of the building — and before they were out of range of security cameras. The pictures of all three men's faces were immediately rushed to media outlets all over the city. "Me and my friend Joey opened the newspaper and said, 'Holy cow! There's Mikey!'," said bartender Bill Stout. He wasn't the only one who recognized the suspects: more than 60 people called police to say they recognized at least one of the men. "Calls are still coming in," a police spokesman said. (AP)

...Some people just don't realize how many friends they have until the chips are down.

Hold This, But Don't Look at It: Secret documents detailing security provisions and potential escape routes from several area prisons were provided to Israeli jail officials. Unfortunately, the documents were in English. The administrators turned the Hebrew translation chore over to their only source of free labor for such time-consuming tasks: their prisoners. A special police unit is investigating. (AFP) *...The Iraqi Republican Guard will be happy to supply assistance.*

Dutch for a Day
President Ford Plugs for Warship
UPI headline

Lickety Split: Rep. Dorothy Pelote of Savannah, Ga., watched with disgust when a bag boy at her grocery store licked his fingers to get a grip on the plastic sacks when bagging her purchases. Rather than speak to the manager, she decided the best thing to do was pass a law requiring stores to provide clerks with "a device designed to wet the fingers" so they wouldn't need to lick them. A sponge would do. Despite calling her anti-spit measure a "common sense health bill," she abandoned the campaign after it got a lot of publicity. (AP) *...She merely came to realize that spit happens.*

Whatever You Say: Is communication the key to a happy marriage? No, says research by the University of Florida. Rather, delusion is a much better solution. "When it comes to marital happiness, it's good to be able to tell yourself a story you'd like to believe," says psychology professor Benjamin Karney, such as convincing yourself that things are getting better and forgetting the hardships of the past. "The advice to husbands and wives to communicate better puts a lot of pressure and blame on couples," he said. "It says, 'If only you communicated better, you'd be happy.' I don't think that's true." (Reuters) *...Just what women* *want to hear: men now have official permission to go back to grunting.*

Step Right Up: Robert Allen Smith is scheduled for execution in Indiana for murder. He is allowed to choose 10 people to witness his death. The state, however, has rejected his method of choosing his 10 witnesses: he wants to sell tickets for $1,000 each, with the proceeds going to a children's charity. "People are fascinated by the death penalty," Smith says. "They love to see violence." (AP) *...The Super Bowls are sufficient, thanks.*

A Crack in her Theory: Brenda Duncan of New Berlin, Wis., was tired of the anti-abortion protesters in front of her house, saying they were harassing her and her children. Her husband, a gynecologist, performs abortions. She admits she called the protesters "asses" and then "showed them what they looked like" by dropping her pants and mooning them. District Attorney Paul Bucher says he plans to file disorderly conduct charges against Duncan. (UPI) *...Next, she plans to call D.A. Bucher a boob.*

Let Me Be Brief: The German army is rethinking underwear. A study found that standard-issue white briefs were being left behind for more appealing styles. "It turned out a lot of soldiers, particularly when they were going out, didn't find them sexy enough or something," a Defense Ministry spokesman said. "So we thought it was a waste of money handing them out in the first place." Instead, recruits who don't want the regular underwear are given a $25 grant to buy whatever kind they want, though the army will still issue olive-green battledress underwear for combat situations. (Reuters) *...Did you really have to make us ponder what camouflage underwear is supposed to hide?*

Debunked: Craig Nancarrow, the tourism director for East London, South Africa, had an idea to entice more visitors to the city aquarium. He had aquarium guide Tessa du Toit, 18, dress up as a mermaid. It indeed brought in 350 visitors curious to see the marvel, but when du Toit refused to go into the water — because she was afraid it would ruin her costume — the crowd grew unruly and started throwing things at her. "Most people who came knew that there is no such thing as a mermaid, but a few who truly believed in it got a bit out of hand when they discovered the truth," du Toit said. "I thought it was a well-known fact that mermaids don't exist," a baffled Nancarrow added. (AP) *...They don't? I suppose next, you'll be telling us humans aren't descended from space aliens.*

Enjoying Earth, Wish You Were Here: The book of Genesis was mistranslated, say followers of the Raelian Church. Humans were not created in God's image, but in the image of space aliens. All the prophets, from Jesus to Mohammed, were space aliens, and these superior beings are ready to return — just as soon as Earth builds them an embassy. "They are from a planet in our galaxy, but not in our solar system," says church member Marie-Helene Parent of Miami, Fla. The church has raised $7 million for the embassy, which they plan to build in Jerusalem by 2035. Or maybe somewhere else: it has to be a place "where there's beautiful weather," she says. (AP) *...After traveling dozens of light years to see how we turned out, their primary concern will be the local weather forecast?*

No Six-Legged Spice: After bouts with food poisoning from "foreign food", the British rock group Spice Girls have decided to hire their own cooks to travel with them when abroad. Each of the five Girls will have her own personal chef, which will cost the group about 250,000 pounds (US$400,000) on their next tour. "If they had to cancel a gig, it would be the most expensive bug anyone has ever had," said a spokesman from their record company. "It would throw the world tour into chaos and cost them a fortune. We really can't risk them getting ill again." (AFP) *...If only they had that much concern for their audience's stomachs.*

There Goes the Neighborhood: In the last 26 years, Dennis Cayse, 50, of Hillsboro, Ohio, has been charged with driving under the influence of alcohol 24 times, with convictions resulting 18 times. He's spent time in prison twice, and has had his driver's license revoked permanently. But that didn't stop him from another drunken spin behind the wheel recently. "He doesn't deny he's an alcoholic," says Judge James Hapner, who has seen Cayse in his courtroom on several occasions. "He just doesn't see that as a problem." Since taking away his driver's license didn't work,

Hapner has ordered Cayse to move his residence to within walk-ing distance of a liquor store or bar. "It's my hope that he'll walk to get his beer and wine rather than drive," Judge Hapner says. (AP) ...*The judge got it almost right: an order forcing Cayse to move to a prison cell for the rest of his life would have fixed the problem more surely.*

Giddy-up: The Society for the Prevention of Cruelty to Animals, which often monitors Hollywood film sets that use animals in TV shows and movies, has ordered that two horses be removed from the show "Dr. Quinn, Medicine Woman", and 30 others had their workloads cut. The SPCA said some horses were being over-worked during the production of the show, and demanded they get more rest. Star Jane Seymour did not return phone calls seeking comment. (AP) ...*She maintains the extra rest order applied to her, too.*

Overachiever: It's easy for teachers at the Satirlar village primary school in southeast Turkey to remember the surname of most of the pupils: 35 of the 70 students have the same last name, because they all share the same father, Ziya Yasar. He has 51 children total, from three wives. The school situation won't change soon. "I've got two more kids who haven't reached school age yet," he said. (Reuters) ...*There's a guy who takes the PTA seriously.*

Overachiever II: Salim Juma Mubarak, 52, has abandoned his attempt to set a record in the United Arab Emirates: he stopped at 49 on his goal of fathering 60 children. His 22 sons and 27 daughters from six wives has created a financial burden since his three current wives insist on maintaining separate houses. (AFP) ...*From each other, from him, or from the kids?*

Make Mine Medium-Rare

Cattleman Grilled by
Oprah's Lawyers

UPI headline

Bull in a China Shop: A thief managed to grab a 19-inch Ming Dynasty platter and a pair of Sung Dynasty vases from the Yanmonoki Museum in Japan. Spotted by a guard, the escaping thief couldn't quite keep hold of it all — he jumped into a waiting car with the vases, worth $38,500, but dropped the platter, where it smashed to bits on the road outside the building. Before it hit the pavement, the 600-year-old Chinese relic was worth $385,000. (AP) ...*Smash and grab, grab and smash, what's the difference?*

Are You a Man or a Mouse? Britain's Human Fertility and Embryology Authority warns: don't buy sperm on the Internet. Though it is already illegal in Britain for anyone to store sperm or "assist in treatment services" without a license, the HFEA says they have found sites on the Internet advertising "unscreened" sperm. "Diseases such as HIV, syphilis or hepatitis can all be contracted from unscreened sperm," they warned. Meanwhile, researcher Roger Short of the Royal Women's Hospital in Melbourne, Australia, has hatched a plan to grow human sperm in mice using tissue transplanted from humans. Short says this would allow technicians to better "monitor" sperm growth and foster research into human infertility. Biologists warn that such a scheme could spread viruses from mice to humans, and even Short admits most people are shocked by his plan. "The first time you say to anyone that we want to produce human sperm in mice, they look at you with frank horror," he said. (Reuters, 2) ...*No sense in letting universal revulsion stand in the way of science.*

Trails of Tears: A robbery at the Dunkin' Donuts in Northbridge, Mass., was pretty easy for police to solve. The robber grabbed a bag of coins as part of his $1,400 of loot, but tore the bag in the process. Officers followed a trail of change from the front door of the shop to a nearby apartment building, where they found the suspect, the money, and the ski mask and weapons used in the robbery. The robbed employee provided the cops with another clue: when the thief addressed him by his nickname, he recognized the robber as a former employee of the store. Meanwhile, the manager of the Swinger Adult Book Store in Anchorage, Alaska, may have had to choke back laughter when he called police after a robbery. The robber didn't just tap the $200 in the till, he took the entire cash register — leaving behind the end of the register tape so that he dragged a trail of paper from the roll in the machine. Police found him three blocks away at the other end of the tape. (AP, 2) *...Go to jail. Go directly to jail. Do not pass 'Go'. Do not collect $200.*

Cheesecake Beefcake: Butcher Kenneth Black is suing the Von's supermarket chain in Southern California after being fired. A female co-worker complained that Black had "intentionally" cut meat to resemble female genitalia, and that complaint led to sexual harassment charges and his dismissal, he says. His lawsuit says the cut of meat in question "had been customarily performed by meat cutters in excess of 20 years, and was commonly regarded as a standard cut of meat at grocery stores," Black's suit says. He adds that in 20 years, he had never had a complaint about the shape of his meat from co-workers, supervisors or customers, and he was simply cutting it as he had been taught. (Reuters) *...Further, Von's says, the skyrocketing sales of beef loin has nothing to do with publicity surrounding the lawsuit.*

To Insure Proper Surliness: When Barbara Mitchell had lunch out one day, she was not pleased with the service. She made a statement by leaving a one-cent tip. "I don't know what happened," claims Oscar Alvarran, the waiter at Trattoria Spiga restaurant in Costa Mesa, Calif. He says he entered ".01" on the credit card machine, but when Mitchell got the bill, the tip showed as $10,000.00. The restaurant apologized and suspended the waiter for a week. "I should have left cash," Mitchell said. (AP) *...Which the waiter would have recognized as a rare 1909s-VDB penny worth several hundred dollars.*

To Insure Peaceful Standoff: Miami, Fla., police had surrounded a house after a man barricaded inside threatened to kill himself. During the tense standoff, a food delivery man walked up to the officers. "This is for the guys surrounding the house," the delivery man said, handing over containers of soup, salad and fish ordered by the man in the house. "This has never happened before," a Miami-Dade Police spokesman said, adding the officers never had time to eat the food. The man surrendered about an hour later and was taken for mental evaluation. (UPI) ...*Good. Soup and fish? For lunch? Clearly insane.*

Call of the Wild: When Lincoln and Dawna DeMarey got into a car accident 100 miles from home, they thought they would never find their cat again after "Precious" ran from the wrecked car into nearby woods. After 19 days of occasional sightings near the Waterville, Maine, crash site, the DeMareys made a recording of familiar sounds: them calling the cat, and the grind of their can opener cutting through the lid of a can of cat food. When the sound of the opener played, Precious ran out of the woods straight for the tape recorder. "We'd given up," Lincoln said. "I'd thrown away all his records and everything." (AP) ...*There goes the old "Your room is just like you left it" line.*

Unfortunately, They're Not Yet Sure What to Feed Them

Report: U.S. Scientists Create "Living Breasts"

Reuters headline

Survival of the Typists: When Valdir Martins Pozza, a machine worker in Brazil, lost the use of his little finger in a job-related accident, a compensation court ruled that he was not entitled to disability benefits. The court ruled "the pinkie serves little use for the hand and ... is considered an appendage that tends to disappear with the evolution of the human species." An appeals court overturned the decision. "The healthy human body has no disposable parts," the appellate judge ruled, awarding Pozza lifetime benefits. (AP) ...*After which Pozza gave the first judge the finger.*

Priorities Set: San Francisco has a new home for the homeless. The $7 million compound has color TVs in every room. "Lots of hugs" for any resident who feels lonely. Special ventilation systems keep the air clean and odorless, and free food is delivered to each room at mealtimes. Even medical and "beauty" care is provided. "We are trying to test the envelope here," says director Richard Avanzino. "What we really hope is that this will help us to save a lot more lives." But hungry humans need not apply: this is the city's new animal shelter. Avanzino defends the opulent dog and cat house, which is even stocked with real furniture. "People think of pets as family members. You wouldn't put your family member in a cage, would you?" (Reuters) ...*Sure some of the endowment would buy a lot of cardboard box homes for homeless street families. However, the pound has cable TV bills to pay.*

Big City Envy: The city of Boulder, Colo., averages just 1.8 murders per year. The still-unsolved killing of child beauty queen JonBenet Ramsey was the city's only murder of 1996. But that high-profile case was just the first of several killings to shake up the relatively small town a half-hour outside Denver. When news of another recent murder reached Stanley Bingham, deputy director of the Boulder Chamber of Commerce, he viewed it as an opportunity. "If there's any justice, this news will zip the lips of our friends in Denver who would have you believe Boulder is some kind of commune for peace-and-love kooks and do-nothing trustfunders," he said. "We're a vital, growing metropolitan area, and nobody can argue with our violent crime statistics." (Boulder Weekly) ...*Once the new smog generators are installed, the city's hellhole conversion process will be complete.*

Loophole: It has been pointed out to the British government that there is no law against cannibalism. But Home Office Minister Alun Michael says there is no need for such a law, so the government will not be bothering to pass one. "If anyone were to attack or kill a person with the intention of eating any part of the victim's body, it would already involve the commission of a criminal offence," he said in a written explanation. (AFP) ...*So to stay clear of the law, make sure they're already dead.*

100,000 Watts, Bulb's Still Dim: Greenville, S.C., disk jockey Paul Breakfield, 30, known on WFBC-FM as "Tom Steele", has been convicted of reckless driving after an on-air publicity stunt. A blindfolded Breakfield drove a radio station van along city streets — and Interstate 385 — as a "tribute" to blind musician Ray Charles. A producer in the passenger seat directed him around obstacles. The DJ was ordered to pay a $200 fine and perform 240 hours of community service, a sentence Breakfield complained was "harsh". (AP) *...Not harsh enough: the judge should make him wear the blindfold around his mouth for that time instead.*

Community Service II: A judge in Swansea, Wales, was listening to the testimony of a 13-year-old girl who said she had been raped by another 13-year-old after a drinking spree. She told the court that she had been drinking Pimm's, a 25 proof alcoholic beverage, neat. "You must have had the mother and father of all hangovers after that," Judge Richard Bougier said. The girl said that was true. So the judge advised her to wait until she is older before she drinks. "But if you can't wait," he counseled, "dilute the drink with one part Pimm's to six parts of lemonade at least." (AFP) *...Charges of underage drinking will be waived upon completion of an advanced bartending course.*

Dim Bulb II: When 23-year-old Michael Gentner's friends dared him to swallow a fish, he accepted the challenge. But it wasn't a goldfish. When paramedics arrived, the tail of the 5-inch fish was sticking out of his mouth, and he was choking. They were not able to clear his airway in time. Akron, Ohio, police have decided not to charge the friends for any crime in the death. "If I dare you to jump off a bridge and you do it, and you're 23 years of age, you're stupid," a police spokesman explained. (AP) *...True, but few have the guts to say it in public anymore.*

Lay Lie: Dutch doctors report in the British Medical Journal that they have developed a new surgical technique "to reconstruct the hymens of adolescent girls who are no longer virgins but wish to appear so." Rotterdam gynecologist Adrian Logsman says the operations are for "immigrant women" from cultures that require brides to be virgins, and that the first patients, aged 16 to 23, were satisfied with the results of the procedure. (Reuters) *... "Of course you're the first, darling! Why do you men all ask the same silly question?"*

Crabby: A Littleton, Colo., seafood restaurant that ended up with a live, 20-year-old lobster decided not to cook the crustacean, but instead use it for a bit of publicity. After keeping it in a tank for several months as a display, the Chowda House restaurant accepted an offer from a United Airlines pilot to fly it back to Boston for release back into the wild. First, one of its claws fell off during the flight, perhaps from the stress of being handled. But the 10-pound beast was dropped back into the water while news cameras rolled. It was when people saw that videotape that the upset really started: the would-be rescuers didn't remove a band holding the other claw safely shut before dropping him into the water. And, they dropped him in an area "teeming" with lobster traps. (AP) *...That's one way to keep the publicity going — just do it again and again!*

It's All Relative: Jonathan M. Charest, 31, was tired of his relatives sharing his Rochester, N.H., apartment. The husband and wife in the spare bedroom argued loudly, Charest said, and he wanted to break it up. He did it with a chainsaw, buzzing through their bedroom door. "It shut them up," Charest told police, who charged him with reckless conduct. After the incident, the couple moved in with a different relative. (AP) *... "They only have a weed-whacker," the couple said. "We feel pretty safe there."*

Who's Your Decorator? A former assistant attorney general was convicted of theft in New Hampshire after he was found to have furnished his home and office with "thousands" of items of stolen art, books and computers from museums and libraries around New England. William McCallum, 34, admitted to 65 counts, but claimed he was not guilty by reason of insanity. A jury rejected his defense. McCallum was sentenced to serve at least two years and fined $2,000. (AP) *...Like any jury would consider him more insane than the average lawyer.*

Balls! A study by Georgia State University finds that lawyers, in general, don't have high levels of testosterone. However, trial lawyers tend to have 30 percent more testosterone in their blood than other lawyers, says psychology professor James Dabbs, who led the study. And, "it was true in both men and women." The tests were even predictive: after measuring the hormone levels in a number of lawyers over several years, those with higher testosterone were more likely to become trial lawyers. It's not necessarily a good thing, however. "They don't win very often. They don't get money. They tend to be in small law firms," Dabbs said. "The really high-class lawyers are not defense lawyers. If you're really good in law school, you don't end up a trial lawyer." The high-testosterone lawyers "just aren't academically inclined." (Reuters) ...*But they sure knew how to party.*

Picky Picky Picky

Israeli Religious Leader Bans Nose Picking on Sabbath

AFP headline

Stupid Is as Lawyer Does: William Lee Monroe, 28, presented a novel defense in his trial for arson. When he moved out of his Fort Worth, Texas, apartment, he stole the flat's refrigerator, light bulbs, and gas stove — but he didn't seal off the gas line, investigators said. The resulting explosion injured five people, two seriously. Monroe's defense: he was too stupid to know that leaking gas was dangerous. "Stupid is as stupid does," offered his defense attorney, Peter Fleury. The jury rejected Monroe's "Forrest Gump Defense" and found him guilty. He faces up to 40 years in prison. (AP) ...*Life is like a box of matches.*

Suburban Legend: Ohio Rep. James Traficant is worried about the Internet. He is urging Congress to protect kids from sexual content online, and says he now has proof of its dangers: a letter from a constituent who says she got pregnant over the net. "That's right, pregnant," he ranted, telling how "Frances" was impregnated via e-mail by a boyfriend 1,500 miles down the wire. "It's time for Congress to act," he claimed. "The Internet needs a chastity chip" to protect online users from "immaculate reception." (Reuters) ...*Jim, the only thing you need to worry about online is remote polling by the smart voters.*

Breast Bauble: Do your earrings attract men's attention to a spot that's ...*well...* too high? Try a Breastee — a décolletage decoration that wedges into your cleavage. With matching earrings, they cost up to $1,500. But if you're not at least a C-cup, forget it, says designer Maybelline Williams. "Some women will need to wear a body enhancer such as a Wonderbra to create a little cleavage," she recommends. But don't blame her too much: she admits she isn't big enough to hold a Breastee in place herself. (Newsweek) *...If she were big enough for one, she'd know she wouldn't need it.*

When You Care Enough to Send the Only Choice: Greeting card giant Hallmark is introducing a sympathy card for people who have lost a friend or relative to suicide. "There was a resounding response for this kind of card, cards that deal with death and dying and spirituality," a spokeswoman said. If the card is successful, the company will consider expanding the line. (AP) *...Meanwhile, how comforting will it be to family members to get 40 copies of the same card?*

Not Tonight, Dear: A study by the National Opinion Research Center at the University of Chicago finds that, in general, better educated people have less sex. Of 10,000 American adults studied, those with "some college" average 61 times per year, and it declines from there, with college grads averaging fewer couplings, and those with graduate degrees even less. Meanwhile, researchers at Johns Hopkins University in Baltimore, Md., say that a survey of 13,345 Americans shows that better-educated people have more tension headaches, with the highest incidence among those who had attended graduate school. (UPI, Reuters) *...Sometimes, it takes a second study to fully understand the results from the first study.*

Cost of Living: A survey by Town & Country magazine found that while 25 percent of average Americans are happy, those who are "rich" — meaning they had incomes of at least $100,000 or savings of at least $200,000 — are twice as likely to describe themselves as happy. "These results fly in the face of everything we've ever heard about money buying happiness," said the magazine's astonished publisher. (UPI) *...Well duh: have you ever seen a Rolls Royce with a bumper sticker proclaiming, "Life Sucks"?*

Last Bid: A foursome playing whist (bridge) in Ipswich, England, say they were all dealt perfect hands. Each player was dealt 13 cards of the same suit, and they are asking the Guinness Book of Records to record the feat. A Guinness spokesman said the odds of one perfect whist hand was about 635 billion to one; the odds of all four players getting perfect hands is 2,235,197,406,895, 366,368,301,599,999 to one. (AFP) ...*Did they calculate the odds of whether the players told the truth?*

Hard to Beat II: Jean-Noel Charolais of Grenoble, France, has beaten a record set by a Swede. Charolais was buried up to his neck in snow, wearing only shorts, for 42 minutes and 31 seconds, beating the Swede's record by three and a half minutes. "When the spirit controls the body, it is much easier to control emotion, stress, shivering and discover the body's other possibilities," he explained. (AFP) ...*Frostbite, necrosis and death, for instance.*

Capitalist Tools: Women who work in the New York securities industry say they've been subject to ongoing sexual harassment, but they can't sue since their industry requires arbitration of legal problems. They report they've been groped, called nasty names, threatened with firing unless they gave sexual favors, and even have had male co-workers unzip their pants and expose themselves. New York Attorney General Dennis Vacco, who listened to the stories in a public hearing, said the evidence gathered at the hearing would be used "primarily as an investigative tool." (Reuters) ...*Funny: that's exactly what the men who exposed themselves said.*

Dope Deceit: Where there is a surprise drug test at work, there's an attempt to beat it. But cheaters don't always get very far with their ploys, such as substituting other liquids for urine. For instance, a Virginia man tried to substitute water from the toilet bowl, which was discovered the moment he handed it over. "He was color blind," the tester said. "He didn't realize the water was blue." Others are a bit more savvy: they'll give samples of the right color, but sometimes it's "dead cold," says the owner of a Texas drug testing firm. "They say, 'What do you mean it's not mine?'" Other drug testing firms note some people thus heat their samples — with a cigarette lighter. "We've had specimens handed back that were too hot to hold onto," says a St. Louis tester. (USA Today) *...But in a nuclear power plant, that may be a sign of something else.*

For I Have Sinned: Andre Lajeunesse said it was the first time he saw a priest in his nude bar. It may be the last time: not only did the 71-year-old Ottawa priest have a heart attack and die as soon as he sat down in a booth for a private show, the Montreal, Quebec, Canada, bar was raided by police the next day. Officers found that in addition to strip shows, the bar offered "sexual services for between 25 dollars (US$17.50) and 80 dollars (US$56), depending on the tastes of the customer." When Ottawa archbishop Monseigneur Marcel Gervais was informed of the circumstances of the Catholic priest's death, he philosophized, "We are all sinners and we are all in need of God's mercy." (AFP) *...Among other services, depending on the tastes of the customer.*

The Case of the Shy Exhibitionist: Police in Pleasanton, Calif., are looking for an unusual flasher: a man who drops photographs of his genitals on the sidewalk for women to find. At least four women have found Polaroid snaps that were dropped in their paths as they walked, police say. "Because of the persistent nature of this, somebody is committing a crime at this point," a police spokesman said. However, while female police officers sent walking through the area as decoys have not turned up any additional pictures, "we have ...a very general description of what the man might look like." (Reuters) *...Tall, thin, bald, and one eye.*

To be Mounted on Alps Ski Resort Gondolas
Italy To Buy 735 Stinger Missiles
AP headline

Fly Me: A survey by Shuttle by United found that 87 percent of business travelers would rather sit next to a co-worker than the boss on airplane flights. "We suspected that business travelers prefer a quiet flight, but it was a surprise to learn that bosses often get passed over when choosing potential seatmates," said Shuttle by United president Amos Kazzaz. (Reuters) *...When asked whether they would mind sitting next to a crying child, 74 percent of business travelers said that's the same thing as sitting next to the boss.*

Hard Headed: George Borden, 57, a fuel truck driver in St. Petersburg, Fla., stopped at a gas station to deliver a load. That's when four men robbed him, forcing him to lie on the ground. After getting $85, one of the robbers stuck his gun to Borden's head and fired. The impact of the bullet slammed his head to the pavement. For good measure, the robber shot him a second time, again in the head. Borden played dead — both bullets had bounced off his skull. He was released from the hospital after 12 quick stitches in his scalp. Doctors told Borden he "was lucky. Lucky, lucky, lucky boy," he said. (UPI) *...It really says something about gas prices when they take the driver's wallet but not any gas.*

Soft Headed: Medical examiners were called in to investigate the case of two dead bodies. They figure it this way: Brian Olesky's friend Elrod Hill, who left a note saying he "wanted to end it all," apparently decided to do it at Olesky's house with an AK-47 assault rifle. Olesky sat next to him on the couch. The high-velocity slug went through Hill's head and hit Olesky, killing him also. (AP) *...It's important to choose the right tool for any job.*

Out of Tune: The classical music community has lost touch with its audience, says cellist Julian Lloyd Webber. Webber, brother of composer Andrew Lloyd Webber, says that the classical music establishment has forgotten about tonality and harmony, leaving that to "the Beach Boys and the Beatles [who] provided people with the harmony they were looking for." The media, too, is to blame, since they ignore classical music "unless semi-naked bimbo violinists...are involved." (Reuters) *...At least someone is catering to the masses.*

Pip Pip, Come Along Now: Ted Oliver, a Briton who has worked for 10 years in the U.S. as a bounty hunter, has a great idea for vacation packages for his countrymen. For just 800 pounds (US$1300) per week, not including expenses, Oliver will give would-be felon chasers a quick lesson in self defense and hand-cuffing techniques, a semi-automatic pistol, a bullet-proof vest, and the chance to back Oliver up on manhunts. Also not included: the tourists will not get a share of any rewards paid for any captured suspects. The British Association of Travel Agents has one suggestion for anyone wanting to go: buy all the insurance you can get your hands on. (AFP) *...And never forget that anything you say can and will be used against you in a court of law.*

Intoxicant Alternatives: Women tired of drunks abusing them shouldn't turn to charming men, says Refuge, a British charity. "The charming man who wines and dines you is just as likely to abuse women," claims Refuge chief executive Sandra Horley. "Is he using his charm to manipulate and control you?" (Reuters) *...Save your life: date a geek today.*

Who's Calling? Chile, which was the first country to establish a permanent base in the Antarctic 50 years ago, is celebrating: after all this time, the base finally got a telephone installed. "Thanks be to God that the firm Entel Chile has donated a telephone," said enthusiastic base commander Lt. Col. Bernardo Orrego. "We are very thankful for it." However, the line has not been connected yet, and Entel was not able to give a time estimate for when it would be working. (Reuters) *...They'll know: it'll ring, during dinner, and a nice man will ask if they'd like to change their long distance carrier.*

Dinner Bell II: The American Association of Retired Persons is planning to "train" seniors on how to hang up on telemarketers so they aren't taken in. AARP says seniors are just too polite to hang up, and then get suckered in by too-good-to-be-true schemes. "We're urging people to end the call quickly," says an AARP spokeswoman. "Use whatever method is comfortable for you to get off the line." They suggest offering excuses such as "I'm just the housekeeper" or "They don't live here anymore." (AP) *...If they're too polite to hang up, won't they be too honest to lie?*

You Belong in the Zoo: A soldier in Cyprus took his girlfriend to the Limassol zoo. As it was 2:45 a.m., it was closed. Authorities said that during the "illicit" visit, the unnamed, 18-year-old soldier "fondled" two caged lions. They bit his hands badly enough he needed surgery. "He was lucky they didn't bite anything else," a police spokesman said. (Reuters) ...*What else was he sticking into the cage?*

That-a-Way: Wild apes make sophisticated travel plans, says Dr. E. Sue Savage-Rumbaugh of Georgia State University. She studied pygmy chimpanzees, or bonobos, in the Congo and found that the animals sent different groups to different destinations in their searches for food, and then met up at the end of the day in a specific location chosen before they left. The apes are probably using symbolic language, she suggests. "A whole tree full of bonobos will work out where they are going to meet," Savage-Rumbaugh said. (UPI) ...*However, when lost, they refuse to stop to ask for directions.*

Take Us To Your Leader: Space aliens speak Croatian. At least, that's the conclusion of Jako Vrancic, a farmer living near Sibenik, Croatia, who said a spaceship with four extraterrestrials landed in his field while he was working. "We had no problem communicating as they spoke a broken form of Croatian," Vrancic said. The farmer offered them lunch, but they weren't hungry, he said, adding, "I felt no fear, as I had previously seen things like this on TV." (Reuters) ...*He must have turned it off before the end, then.*

Listen to Freddie: Despite 18 years of experience working at a Florida fishing camp, Freddie Padgett was afraid of water. So much so that he wore a life jacket to bed on stormy nights, just in case a tornado picked him up and dropped him in the lake. Too paranoid for description? Well, Padgett, sleeping inside a recreational vehicle near Geneva, was blown into Lake Harney by a tornado spawned by the recent string of thunderstorms vexing central Florida. He was spotted several hours later by a sheriff's helicopter a mile away from his RV, still floating. He suffered broken ribs and other injuries, but the life jacket probably saved his life, authorities say — especially considering the fact that another man at the fishing camp, also torn from his RV, has not yet been found. (UPI) *...To be forever remembered at the camp as "the big one who got away."*

Sheepskin
Harvard Gets Two-Ply Toilet Tissue
AP headline

No Deposit, No Return: A man stopped by the Wachovia Bank in Atlanta, Ga., to cash a check, then returned later to rob the place. When the teller saw that the man's robbery note was written on the back of a completed application for a duplicate Social Security card, she didn't hand it back when he fled. It included his name, address, and Social Security number. "I believe the FBI won't have any trouble finding him," a police spokesman said. (Atlanta Journal-Constitution) *...Good: he's probably lost.*

Who's That Knocking at My Door? Harold Overbeek is angry at the Grand Rapids, Mich., police department. Overbeek had complained that the police needed to clear drug dealers out of his neighborhood. But later, while the 72-year-old man was watching "Law and Order" on TV, a police SWAT team crashed through his front door, threw him on the floor, and accused him of being a drug dealer. The city now says it was all a big mistake: an informant apparently gave police the wrong address. Overbeek's main complaint: "They never said they were sorry," he says, so he's suing the department, alleging his rights were violated. (UPI) *...Punitive damage awards mean never having to say you're sorry.*

Squealer: Pam and Fred Abma of Ramsey, N.J., are lucky to be alive. Their house caught fire, and it was only their pet pot-bellied pig, Honeymoon, that alerted them to the flames. "That little pig saved our lives," Pam gushed. "Honey was the only one who smelled the smoke. The dogs were clueless." Fred agreed. "Pigs are a lot smarter than dogs, clearly," he said. (Reuters) *...Not necessarily: who wants to eat a raw pig?*

Class Dismissed: After Chaquita Doman, a 5-year-old kindergarten student at Edgewater Elementary in Pensacola, Fla., allegedly bit her school counselor hard enough that the wound required stitches, police took out a warrant charging the child with battery of an elected official or educator, a felony, and told her parents to surrender the girl for booking. The girl's outraged father calls the charges "ludicrous". (AP) ...*Clearly someone in this case is bananas.*

If You Can't Beat 'em, Join 'em: Britain's Ministry of Defence is planning to decriminalize adultery in the ranks. Under proposed new rules, extramarital affairs between soldiers and civilians — "but not each other" — will be allowed, the Ministry says. A spokesman said recent scandals have convinced the military that society has changed since the no-sex rules were implemented, and trying to punish affairs is "unrealistic". However, the Ministry adds, homosexuality will still be a court-martial offense, even though foreign espionage service MI6 "reportedly sent its first gay couple abroad." (AFP) ...*What an inappropriate gift! They should have sent a guy.*

I Know You Are, But What Am I? Earl Kaufmann runs a tattoo parlor in Tucson, Ariz. Calling his body an artist's canvas, it's 80 percent covered in tattoos. But when a competing shop made a less-than-veiled reference to him as a "Scary Guy" in a newspaper ad, Kaufmann didn't get mad, he turned it to his advantage. He legally changed his name to "The Scary Guy", resulting in huge press coverage. "It's an ironic name change, because he's not scary," says his wife, Judy. "He's the sweetest guy you'll ever know." (AP) ...*Easy for you to say, Judy, considering your name is now "Mrs. Scary Guy".*

We the People: A survey by American University's Center for Congressional and Presidential Studies finds that there is wide acceptance of the Internet by Washington politicians. Most representatives have a public e-mail address so constituents can voice their opinions to their elected officials, but few use it to respond. Instead, they expect constituents to include their postal addresses for a paper response. Why? The survey found that Congressional staffers think people would be dissatisfied with e-mail responses, and instead surely prefer replies printed on Congressional letterhead. (Washington Post) ...*That's only because the paper is worth more than the promises written on it.*

We the People II: "There are a few that take advantage of the system to make themselves look good at the expense of the city because they know the system will protect them," explains Bruce Rider, 42, of Plainview, Texas. He's running for town mayor, promising that he will not campaign for the position and, if elected, he promises he will refuse to take office. By running against the otherwise-unopposed incumbent, Rider is costing the town an extra $8,400 in election costs. If he wins and refuses to take office, the town will have to hold an even more expensive special election to replace him. "I'm giving the average citizen a forum," he claims. "Sometimes the only battles worth fighting are the ones you can't win." (Lubbock Avalanche-Journal) ...*"Democracy is the theory that the common people know what they want, and deserve to get it good and hard." —H.L. Mencken (1880–1956), U.S. journalist.*

The "Openness in Government" Thing
Taken to its Logical Extreme

C.I.A. Drafts Covert Plan to Topple Saddam

New York Times headline

Squall Line: California's coast is being hit hard by storms blamed on the "El Niño" ocean current. Locals can hardly hear a weather report without being told El Niño is at work. The phone rings a lot at Al Nino's house. Nino, who is listed in the telephone directory, says people call at all hours. "It's always something like, 'Why are you doing this?'," Nino says. While the retired Navy man doesn't enjoy being awakened in the middle of the night, "I usually joke around with them a bit," he says, telling callers he controls the weather because "I didn't really have nothing else to do." (AP) ...*There are no dumb questions, just dumb people asking questions.*

Help Wanted: Lauren and Ashton Mills know their mother is dying of cancer. The 10-year-old twins from Oxford, England, not wanting to be placed with a random foster family when the time comes, have advertised for a new family in the local newspaper. "Kids and dog for hire," the ad in the "Situations Vacant" category read. "Life term contract." However, the girls aren't interested in pity. "Sad gits need not apply," the ad warned. Thousands of people have responded. (Reuters) ...*If they're anything like the typical people who reply to singles ads, don't bother, kids!*

When You're Forced to Send the Very Best: York, Pa., Common Pleas Court Judge Sheryl A. Dorney wants to be sure that Leroy Howard Murray Jr. thinks about his crime now and then. Murray, who pleaded guilty to stealing a car stereo, was ordered to send the judge a birthday card each August 21 during his 23-month probation, as well as pay restitution to the victim. (AP) ...*Your honor, here's your birthday greeting / Better by mail than face-to-face meeting / There is no gift, just this two-bit card / I'm only sending it to avoid time that's hard.*

Census: Doctors in Mexico caused an international news flurry when they announced recently that a woman was pregnant with nine babies. Later, the publicity fury lessened when they said no, it was seven. Cristina Hernandez has now given birth — to six babies, all in good health. (Reuters) ...*In the U.S., most doctors can accurately count up to 10 — 20 if they take their shoes off.*

Tiny Bubbles: The Kloster brewery in Neuzelle, Germany, has introduced a beer concentrate specifically for bathing. Four three-quart bottles of concentrate, at $22 each, when mixed with water, fill a 32-gallon tub. The biggest difference between the bath beer and the regular variety is the yeast has been left in, which is "soothing to the skin" and a good treatment for eczema, the brewer claims. And, "You can bathe in it, or drink it," he said. "Whoever wants to can do both." (AP) ...*Best of all, it makes the bath drown-proof: the deeper you go, the higher you get.*

Yes, Dear: If you want your marriage to be successful, forget trendy communication methods like "active listening", says John Gottman of the University of Washington. Psychologist Gottman and his team studied 130 newlyweds and compared them with long-married couples to see how they handled disagreements. "We found that only those newlywed men who are accepting of influence from their wives are winding up in happy, stable marriages," Gottman said. (Reuters) ...*While their research results didn't support this conclusion, they were afraid not to write what their wives told them to.*

Minuteman: Senator Edgardo Angara, running for vice president of the Philippines, was out shaking hands with voters to drum up support in the upcoming elections. But when Angara thrust his arms into the crowd, one of the voters pulled his watch off his wrist and ran. (AFP) ...*Turnabout is fair play.*

Expanding Market: London International Group has announced a joint venture with China to provide condoms to the world's most populous country. China already produces 1.2 billion condoms per year, but that's only enough output to provide one to each citizen per year. However, a spokeswoman said, flavored condoms, which are popular in Asia, are not part of the deal, even though "mint condoms go down well in Southeast Asia." (Reuters) ...*"Go down" being a technical term in that business.*

Pot Shot: When Verline Stiffic was asked to come to the office of Brinkley Middle School in Jackson, Miss., because her 15-year-old son was caught with marijuana on campus, she was apparently very unhappy. "She went into the school and started talking to her son," a police spokesman said. "Apparently, the conversation didn't go very well so she pulled out a gun and shot at him." She missed, and has been arrested. (AP) ...*He wouldn't believe her when she said using drugs could kill him.*

The Other Berkley: Police in Berkley, Mich., say that during lunch, "dozens" of students would walk to a house near their school to smoke marijuana and buy pot from two teenaged boys that lived there. After the raid, police talked to the boys' mother, who was apparently unconcerned with the activity in her home.

"It's OK," she told police. "I was raised in the '60s." She was arrested too. (UPI) ...*Same trap, different mice.*

As it is on Earth: When David Justice got a traffic ticket in Gunnison, Colo., he thought of a novel way out: he told the court that he was an ambassador from the Kingdom of Heaven, and as such only the U.S. Supreme Court could rule on his case, per the Constitution. The Colorado Court of Appeals, however, didn't buy it. "We are not aware of any declaration by the Department of State that the Kingdom of Heaven is a recognized sovereign," the court ruled. (Denver Post) ...*No doubt if they sent an ambassador, someone would kill him.*

Wasn't that the General Idea?
Man Dies After Life Support Removed
AP headline

Thou Shalt Not Steal: A survey in Chicago has revealed the most-stolen books from area libraries: the Bible and the Koran. Next are study guides to police and military entrance examinations. (UPI) ...*Certainly no one can expect people to have morals* ***before*** *they study.*

Thou Shalt Not Steal II: Retired Cottonwood, Ala., Police Chief Eugene Coker was on a fishing trip in nearby Malone, Fla., when he saw three armed men put on masks and walk into a bank. He borrowed a rifle and waited for them to come out. "I had it on his head. I had him dead to rights," Coker, 69, said. "He hadn't shot nobody, so I lowered it and shot him in the butt." The suspect limped to the getaway car, so Coker shot a hole in its gas tank. "They never got four blocks." When the car rolled to a stop the three men, identified as local college students, were arrested and charged with bank robbery. (AP) ...*Florida fishing licenses sure are comprehensive.*

Huh? An Australian performance artist has announced plans for his latest artistic feat: he will grow an extra ear. "Stelarc" says that a plastic surgeon will insert "a little rubber balloon" under his skin. "It will be inflated over the period of a month or so to leave a packet of excess skin," the 53-year-old man explained. "Then I will put in an ear scaffold beneath the skin. What you will have is a third ear." (AFP) ...*He'll need more than that if he expects to hear any applause.*

There Goes the Neighborhood: God will return to Earth March 31 — according to followers of God's Salvation Church. But He won't appear just anywhere, they say. Specifically, He'll show up at 3513 Ridgedale Drive in Garland, Texas. "This will happen," says Heng-ming Chen, who moved from Taiwan with 140 followers for the event. "I would stake my life on it." Chen and company have purchased about 30 houses in the area to ensure front-row seats. Neighbors are afraid of what could happen "if God pulls a no-show," thinking back to the Heaven's Gate cult suicide a year before. Police are taking a wait-and-see approach, but are asking TV networks how many satellite trucks to expect on The Day. "Whether God shows up or not, we know there are still going to be a lot of press out here and we're getting ready," a police spokesman said. (AP) ...*Don't let Dan Rather in. He'll claim his own presence fulfills the prophecy.*

I'm Sorry, Dave: A computer designer at the Massachusetts Institute of Technology says she has made advances toward computers with "heart". Rosalind Picard says her new computers will be "beyond human" in friendliness and empathy. Picard says current computers "are like autistics. They have a lot of verbal and mathematical skills, but they really don't have any emotional skills." (UPI) ...*We don't want computers with hearts. We want computers with brains.*

Call in the Stunt Double: At 83, you might think Nilo Silvi of Rome would be enjoying a retired life of leisure. But the Italian pensioner is ready to start a new career after a talent scout spotted him in a disco with his grandson. The scout asked him if he would mind "making a film with beautiful young girls." The scout is a producer of pornographic movies, but that doesn't give Silvi any problems. "We talked about the possibility of filming some group scenes. I said I was willing," he assured the filmmakers. "I'm not ashamed at all." However, Silvi does have two concerns: "I won't use a condom," and, after considering how many sex scenes he might have to perform in, he worried, "Will I have to pay?" (Reuters) *...No: no one said life was fair.*

Fire Up the Students: The Los Angeles Unified School District board has voted to arm their school police force with shotguns. The officers, who already carry sidearms, say they needed the extra firepower because they spend so much time in gang areas. The district will buy 75 shotguns and provide extra firearms training for the officers. "This was long overdue," said a relieved school police spokesman. (AP) *...Forget shotguns. The cops won't be safe until their firepower at least matches what the kids carry.*

Genesis 3:16: Canadian Lesli Szabo, 44, is suing her doctors and McMaster Hospital for $2.4 million because she had pain while giving birth. The Hamilton, Ont., woman claims her doctors told her the birth would be "so pain-free, she could knit or read a book during the procedure." But she said her pain so traumatized her that she had "intrusive thoughts," such as an unfounded belief that the hospital had called her dentist to tell him to make sure "I have as much pain as possible during dental treatment," she testified. Szabo, whose husband is a physician at McMaster, said she filed the suit "to make sure this doesn't happen to anyone else." (Toronto Star) *...Maybe it was something she ate.*

Going, Going, Gone: An auction to sell miscellaneous items which once belonged to John F. Kennedy did not bring in as much money as expected. A wooden plank from the JFK's inaugural podium was estimated to sell for $10,000 to $15,000, but brought just $2,875. A page of doodles JFK drew the day before he was assassinated was expected to bring $30,000 to $40,000, but sold for $11,500. A number of items didn't sell at all, such as his desk and a "Cuban Missile Crisis" paperweight. (Reuters) *...I knew Jack Kennedy. Jack Kennedy was my president. Jack Kennedy was no Jackie Onassis.*

Not Counting Popcorn
Average Movie Cost Reaches $53.4M
AP headline

Save the Dollars: An investigation by the Chicago Tribune has found that several U.S.-based charities formed to "sponsor" and help feed poor children in third-world countries are "rife with scams". Organizations such as Save the Children and Childreach, the newspaper says, do not always send donations directly to needy children as they claim. The paper anonymously sponsored several children for two years, then made surprise visits to their villages. In one village they found a 44-year-old teacher who was hired to write the letters local children were supposed to send to their sponsors. In some cases, they found the sponsored children had been dead for years, but the sponsors had no idea, apparently because the letters were still arriving regularly. (AFP) ...*See? We told you that this poor child hadn't eaten in a long time!*

Save the Pennies: A private investigator has advised the U.S. Senate Subcommittee on Technology, Terrorism and Government Information of a major terrorist threat facing the country: cents-off supermarket coupons. "To terror organizations hiding in our communities, the coupon inserts mean financing, here and abroad," claims Ben Jacobson. He says that terror groups are clipping coupons from newspapers and fraudulently redeeming them to help finance terrorist operations, and it's imperative for the country to toughen coupon fraud laws. (UPI) ...*Help fight terrorism: pledge to pay only full price for Cap'n Crunch.*

Cop Rock: When Oakland, Calif., police officers arrested Julian Aldarondo for allegedly stealing a cookie, Aldarondo says the cops subjected him to "excessive force". Specifically, he says, they made him sit and listen while an officer sang "Escape, The Pina Colada Song", which he alleged was "the most degrading and humiliating experience" of his life. Officer Anthony Toribio said he sang the song to "defuse tension" over the arrest after he found out that Aldarondo was a singer. "It's a snappy song with one of those catchy tunes," Toribio said. The Oakland Police Review Board rejected the excessive force claim. (Reuters) *...Aldarondo has denied reports that, if convicted, he will adopt "Wasting Away in Margaritaville" as his jailhouse theme.*

Off to the Showers: British football referees have a limit to the amount of abuse they will take before they pull out their dreaded red card. So when Melvin Sylvester lost his temper at an amateur game in Charlton and punched out a player, out came the red card. But the card came out of Sylvester's own pocket. He was the referee at the game, and he pulled the card on himself, ejecting himself from the game. "I was sorely provoked," he said later. But Sylvester feels bad enough about the incident that he says he's making his expulsion permanent, and will never officiate at a match again. (AFP) *...Don't you just hate refs who go straight to the red card without even having the courtesy of giving a warning first?*

Terror from Above: British evangelist John Holme says he saw Heaven over Salisbury, England. He decided to get a closer glimpse of his final reward, and while he was at it spread The Word, by flying over the town in a motorized paraglider armed with a megaphone. "I thought that maybe if they heard this voice booming out from the sky, they would think it was God," Holme said later. Witnesses said Holme was veering around trees and fences with a look of "sheer horror in his eyes", but the parapreacher said he wasn't afraid. "Considering it was the first time I had flown, I think my performance was not too bad," he told a reporter. A local magistrate was not amused. He fined Holme 1,050 pounds (US$1,730) plus court costs for flying too close to a populated area. "I can't believe I've got a criminal record after this," lamented Holme. (Reuters) *...Coming this fall from BBC: the new zany sequel to "The Flying Nun".*

Hot Hot Hot: The Firefighters Historical Society in Winnipeg, Manitoba, Canada, are planning a new museum in town to hold their antique fire equipment and memorabilia. They even have a site: an old firehouse. However, the building does not meet fire codes. The Society is raising money to bring it up to current standards, but they had better hurry: the building is the third firehouse on the site. The first two burned down. (AP) *...The third time's the charm.*

Shortcut: A northern California company says addresses on the Internet are too long, too complex, and too hard to remember and type. So the company, centraal, has released a new product that allows a lengthy "URL", such as http://www.thisistrue.com/books.html, to be replaced with simple key words. Their demonstration: replacing a lengthy address for a Walt Disney web page with the keyword "Bambi". But when reporters and customers tried the example keyword, they were not shown a doe-eyed cartoon deer, but doe-eyed live dears on a pornographic site. "THIS AIN'T DISNEY, BOYS!" complained one irate user. "I think I might not use the Bambi example anymore," sheepish company president Keith Teare told reporters. (Reuters) *...That's nothing: you should see "Thumper".*

Mother May I: Paint shop owner Allan Gordon of Alford, Scotland, is "fed up." A new sign posted in front of the shop reads, "We will not supply husbands with coloured paint without a signed note from their wives." Gordon says in the past, men wouldn't pay attention to their wives' instructions on what color to bring home. But now, "men are thinking a bit harder about what they buy." (Reuters) *...Or thinking about telling their wives to buy their own bloody paint.*

Official Scorecard Shows 53,297 Down, Just 1,946,703 to Go

Poll: 2 Million Women Fantasize about Clinton

UPI headline

Mental Exercise: Manchester (England) Metropolitan University sports psychologist Dave Smith says his research shows that thinking about doing exercise helps build muscles, even if you never actually get around to actually doing the exercise. "The brain activity when you imagine doing something vividly, with all the feeling you would get if you did it, is very, very similar to what occurs when you actually do it," he said. (Reuters) *...To check the validity of this theory, vividly imagine yourself having sex.*

Can You Dig It? Police in Nashville, Tenn., saw people leaving a house with boxes of marijuana. They searched the house and found 120 pounds of pot and $100,000 in cash. They also found an interesting piece of paper. "We came across a treasure map," a police spokesman said. "It told us where to dig" at another house the suspects owned. Using a backhoe, officers found $2.8 million in cash buried in plastic containers, plus another $1 million in a commercial storage locker. (AP) *...Better check their mattresses, too.*

Overdrawn: The teller at Marine Midland Bank in Pearl River, N.Y., was confused over the note the man in line had handed her. The man, wearing a plastic bag over his head, handed it over without saying a word. She scratched her head a bit, then asked another teller if she could read it. By the time they decoded the first part — "I've got a gun" — the man had run off. The rest of the note is "still open to conjecture," a police detective said. "It demands money and says he has a gun, but we have to spend some more time with it" to figure out the rest. (AP) *... "Please hurry, I am suffocating in here."*

Boo: A family in Upper Mayfield, England, has been given the go-ahead to pursue a lawsuit against the people that sold them a 250-year-old house because, they charge, the sellers failed to disclose that the house is haunted. The family says they have tried five different exorcism rituals in the house, but they are still subject to being touched by unseen spirits and a feeling of an "evil presence". (AFP) *...In the U.S., we call those insurance salesmen.*

Ahead of his Time: The U.S. Postal Inspection Service has arrested Lawrence Cusack Jr. of Fairfield, Conn., charging him with forgery. Cusack has sold about 700 pages of documents since 1993 supposedly signed in 1961 by President John F. Kennedy, his brother Robert Kennedy, or Marilyn Monroe. Cusack said he obtained the papers from his late father, who was Monroe's mother's lawyer. Authorities were tipped off because of the Zip Code printed on his father's stationery. The U.S. Postal Service didn't introduce Zip Codes until 1963. (UPI) ...*Well, that and the Richard Nixon stamps on the envelopes.*

With This Signature, I Thee Wed: Jose Luis Ferreira, 31, and Eva Maria Alvedro, 24, of La Coruna, Spain, are marrying, but they're not yet sure if it's a lifetime commitment. They've signed a short-term marriage contract, with an option to renew. After two years, the couple will reevaluate the pairing and will then decide whether to sign on for a longer hitch. (AFP) ...*The only amazing part is that the Americans didn't think of it first.*

Dam It! The International Joint Commission says a number of dams and dikes along the U.S./Canadian border are inadequate and could be hazardous. The study especially concerns the Commission's Canadian co-chair, Leonard Legault. "Many of these structures are getting older and we think that continuing vigilance and maintenance are absolutely essential," he said. (AP) ...*We'd appreciate your pointing out exactly which ones are getting younger.*

Just Looking: Britain's Queen Elizabeth II is believed to have made history recently by making her first "official" visit to a pub, the Bridge Inn in Topsham. She declined a pint of ale that the innkeeper offered. A few days earlier, she had visited a supermarket for the first time. She stopped at a store in Oasis Lakeland Forest Village and chatted with the cashier and customers. However, the cashier notes, she did not buy anything. (AFP, 2) ...*The shopowners' association, noting the frequent visits without purchases, are advising clerks that in the future, they should check the Queen's pockets and handbag before letting her leave.*

I Know You Are, but What Am I? Researchers at Ohio State University find that gossip has a "boomerang" effect: the things you tell people about someone are also attributed to you, they say. In other words, if you describe someone as rude and dishonest, people you talk to will also consider you rude and dishonest. "Politicians who allege corruption by their opponents may themselves be perceived as dishonest, critics who praise artists may be perceived as talented, and gossips who describe other's infidelities may be viewed as immoral," said OSU Prof. John Skowronski, who worked on the research. (UPI) ... *Wow, those researchers sure are intelligent and erudite!*

Going Down: Dwayne Brown, 24, figured he could break out of his jail cell on the 18th floor of the Middlesex County (Mass.) Courthouse if he were armed. Police say he told his girlfriend to wait on the street, and he would make a rope out of bed sheets, lower it down to the street from a jail window, and hoist up a gun she would tie to the end. Police were watching as he snaked the rope out the window — but it only reached down to the 14th floor. "It would be funny, [except] when you think about a loaded handgun going to an inmate," said a district attorney spokesman. How did police know the attempt would take place? They overheard Brown making the plans over the jail's telephone. (AP) ...*And some people doubt that police work can be fun.*

Mom Disavows Knowledge of Your Actions: Three teenaged boys have been arrested in Medina, Ohio, after planning a "Mission: Impossible" burglary, investigators say, copying tactics seen in the hit movie about secret agents. The boys planned every minute detail of the crime, using stopwatches and head-mounted flashlights, but they didn't plan on two details. First, "They planned to use a cinder block to break through the glass door," a sheriff's spokesman said. "But after they hit the glass once, twice, three whacks, four and five without breaking through, they apparently realized they had made too much noise and left." And, second, deputies had learned of the plot and had the boys surrounded before they could get away. (UPI) ...*Real intelligence agents remember there's such a thing as counter-intelligence.*

All Hands Off Deck

Hooters Off-Limits to Coast Guard

AP headline

Lack of Evidence: The jury in a Seattle, Wash., drug case is suspected of stealing $1,041 in cash, part of the evidence in the case. Prosecutors gave all the evidence to the jury to take into deliberations, including the money. But when the panel returned from lunch, the cash was gone. Only the jury, the bailiff, and the court clerk had access to the room, a police detective said, adding "there is little doubt in my mind that there was someone on the jury who absconded with the money." However, he said, it's unlikely the case will be solved "unless someone wants to unburden their soul." A mistrial was declared in the case. (Seattle Times) *...It's surprising things like this don't happen more often, considering criminals are entitled to "juries of their peers".*

The Smell Test: Alan Hirsch of the Smell and Taste Treatment and Research Foundation of Chicago wants to know what odors turn people on. He has been subjecting volunteers to various odors while measuring genital blood flow to gauge their sexual arousal. Hirsch says women are turned off by cherries, barbequed meat, and men's cologne. Like men [see *This is True: Deputy Kills Man With Hammer*], women are apparently aroused by the smell of lavender and pumpkin pie, and also cucumbers and baby powder. But the most arousal in women was elicited by the odor of Good 'n' Plenty candy. (Reuters) *...The women apparently didn't realize that "Good 'n' Plenty" is a trademark, not a warranty.*

What's in a Name? A study by the University of California at San Diego finds that people whose initials spell out negative words don't live as long as people whose initials spell out positive words. "It's a little tiny depressant to be called PIG, or a little tiny boost to your esteem to be called ACE or WOW," says psychologist Nicholas Christenfeld. The research found 11 especially "good" sets of initials and 19 particularly "bad" ones, and showed those with better initials such as ACE or GOD lived an average of 4.48 years longer than a control group with neutral initials. Those with worse initials such as DIE or BUM died 2.8 years sooner than the control group, "the notion being that accidents aren't really accidents," Christenfeld said. "Whether deliberate or not, if you think less of yourself, you may be more likely to drive your car into a bridge abutment." (AP) *...BAD you are, ACE I be; I'll be here, while you RIP.*

What's in a Name II: Sailors in the British Navy want "tougher" names for their ships. An anonymous letter sent by seamen on the warship Brave to a military newspaper complained about new ships being christened Ocean, Albion and St. Albans. "This has got to stop," the letter demanded. "It's bad for morale and presents a poor impression on overseas visits." They have suggestions for the top brass: "We recommend Dreadnought, Dauntless, Dominant, Devastation, Defender, Dragon, to be followed by the second batch of E Class — Excalibur, Enforcer, Emperor, Endeavour, Exultant and Extreme." (AP) *...It could be worse: Britain could have spacecraft named after fictional television starcruisers.*

Hair-Raising: If you can't afford to travel in space, maybe you'll want your hair to go. That, at least, is what Encounter 2001 hopes, noting there's only space for hair from 4.5 million people on their spacecraft, scheduled for launch this fall on a trajectory that will take it out of the solar system. For $5,000, the company will launch three to six strands of your hair and some of your "thoughts" on a "high-density" CD in the hopes that the payload will be found in the future by an alien civilization. Then, perhaps, the aliens might be motivated to recreate you from the DNA they find in your hair. As for the CD, "If an alien race is capable of finding the spacecraft, they should be able to access the data," a spokesman said. (Reuters) *...Future tabloid headline: "I Was Resurrected by an Alien Disk Jockey".*

Cutting Class: Each year, the Carroll County (Ohio) Human Services Department gives school teachers a small gift imprinted with an abuse hotline number to promote the state's Child Abuse and Neglect Awareness Month. But when the department's director announced that this year's gift to teachers would be a pocketknife, school administrators balked. "We're not going to outfit the teachers with knives," complained school Superintendent Michael Maiorca. Human Services Director Chris Adams says he'll think of something else for the gift this year. (AP) *...Bulletproof vests.*

Thou Shalt Not: Mitchell Johnson, the 13-year-old boy arrested after an ambush shooting at Westside Middle School in Jonesboro, Ark., that left five students and one teacher dead, is "scared", his attorney said. "He's a little boy," attorney Tom Furth lectured. While Furth says Johnson is young, he "absolutely understands the difference between right and wrong," and has been spending his time in jail reading, including "an awful lot of Bible study." (AP) *...If Furth thinks Johnson is scared now, wait until the kid reads in that Bible what happens to murderers.*

Redress: The German government has drafted a bill to overturn the findings of Third Reich "Racial Purity Courts", which ruled that 350,000 citizens were "feeble-minded", deaf or blind, and should not be allowed to reproduce. Virtually all were forced to undergo sterilization. As of 1996, 50,000 victims were still alive and continued to be discriminated against, they say. (AFP) *...The new law won't be truly fair unless it also applies to the descendants of the victims who have already died.*

Bounceback Inevitable

World Rubber Body Unlikely to Make Major Changes

Reuters headline

Bend Over a Page: "He's not the best role model for young people," said a page — essentially, an intern — for the Iowa state senate. He was explaining why, when the pages had their group photograph taken in the senate chamber, they took down the portrait of President Clinton so it couldn't be seen in the background. "It was a majority consensus to remove his picture for our group picture." (AP) *...You know it's getting bad when proud parents exclaim over their newborns, "Maybe someday he'll grow up to be a Special Prosecutor!"*

Now now now now! Nagging works. That's the conclusion of marketing researchers who found that children get what they want if they nag their parents effectively. The firm studied 150 mothers through 10,000 nagging incidents and found that nagging by children aged 3 to 8 was the reason behind 46 percent of toy purchases by their mothers, as well as 34 percent of movie theater visits and 34 percent of food purchases. While whining "I want it!" didn't work terribly well, reasoned pleadings such as "Mom, Barbie needs a dream house so she can build a family" were found to be more effective. (Reuters) ...*That, and "If you don't buy me this, sympathetic juries of the future will certainly take it into consideration."*

There Must Be 50 Ways to Leave Your Lover: Joel Hines Jr. decided he didn't really want to marry his fiance, Thelma Jones, so he decided to fake the "until death do you part" bit early. He staged an accident on his fishing boat, then snuck off and hopped a bus to Texas. He thought better of the gag when he found out that the Pender County (N.C.) Sheriff's Department had spent five days searching for him in the Northeast Cape Fear River. He turned himself in to the sheriff, who said Hines will not charged with any crime. However, they do want him to pay $5,000 to reimburse the department for the fruitless search for his body. (AP) ...*Maybe he can sell her engagement ring to raise the cash.*

The Hole Truth: When Japan hosted the Winter Olympics in Nagano, local companies were so proud of an innovative new product that they supplied them free to the athletes: condoms made out of polyurethane instead of rubber. Since then, sales have been so good that Sagami Rubber Industries Co. has had a difficult time meeting demand. However, government tests show that more than one percent of samples tested have holes large enough to leak water. "The product has been at the center of attention and we feel very much responsible for consumers," said an embarrassed company spokesman announcing a recall. "We take it upon ourselves to pinpoint the cause." (AFP) ...*I think I've found the problem.*

One for the Road: Lakewood (Wash.) Municipal Judge Ralph H. Baldwin accepted the jury's verdict in a drunk driving case, then turned to more pressing business. "I know this is uncommon, and kind of funny following a [driving under the influence] case," witnesses quoted him as saying, but the judge invited the jury, prosecutor and defense attorney to join him in drinking a 12-pack of beer he stepped out to buy while the jury deliberated. The lawyers and two jurors joined the judge in the jury room for a "cold one". Afterward, he told them "I might as well drink and drive, I do it all the time anyway," and got in his car with an open beer and drove away. "When I saw [my remarks] put down on paper, it looked awful," Judge Baldwin said later. "When I thought about it, I thought, 'Oh my God, you fool'." The judge has resigned. (AP) *...And thus went his nickname from "The Hanging Judge" to "The Hangover Judge".*

One for the Road II: "The municipal police were drunk and attacked a military convoy," Guerrero state (Mexico) governor Angel Aguirre reported at a news conference. "The soldiers repelled the attack, resulting in one policeman dead and another injured." But the mayor of the unnamed rural town disputes the governor's version of the story. He says the drunken police were merely firing their guns randomly, and were not trying to hit the passing convoy. (Reuters) *...But only because they couldn't see well enough to aim.*

Your Lucky Day: Steven Jay Russell has been caught. Again. The Texas convict has escaped from jail three times. Jailers call him "Houdini" and "King Con", the latter because of the method he uses to get out: he convinces authorities he is someone else. In 1996, he impersonated a judge and ordered his own bail reduced. He has also posed as an FBI agent and a doctor. Jailers are confident they can hold him at least for a while: Russell always escapes on Friday the 13th, and there isn't another one for seven months. (UPI) *...The headline: "Inmate mistakes calendar for sieve."*

You Can Fight City Hall: After Glendale, Colo., Mayor Joe Rice pushed through a law to restrict two local strip clubs in the town of 4,000 "low-income" people, voters didn't get mad, they got even. The law raised the minimum age for dancers and required a six-foot buffer zone between dancers and patrons — which would prohibit the audience from stuffing tips into the dancers' G-strings. Angry locals got behind a grass-roots campaign that swept pro-strip-club candidates into all three open seats in a recent city council election, stunning the mayor. One of the first items on the new council's agenda: repeal of the new anti-strip club law, which has not yet gone into effect. (AP) ...*Last year's political activist: "Soccer Mom". This year's political activist: "Joe Sixpack".*

Operation Fishbowl: The Biundo family agreed to live for a month in a department store window in view of passers-by in Zurich, Switzerland, in exchange for 10,000 Swiss francs (US$6,600) as part of a publicity stunt. But the family — a 31-year-old man, his 42-year-old wife, and two daughters aged 11 and 3 — couldn't take the crowds of onlookers and quit after just three days. Television personality Frank Baumann, one of the sponsors of the display, called it a success anyway, saying the experiment "proved" people are "naturally voyeurs". The family will still get the money, plus they've been given a two-week vacation "to recover from the ordeal." (AFP) ...*It have been cheaper to demonstrate voyeurism if they simply hired exhibitionists.*

Learned the Power of the 'bone from Clinton

Canada's Chretien Woos Liberals with Trombone

Reuters headline

Dirty Laundry: Kmart is recalling talking children's T-shirts because of what they say out loud. The shirts show the "Sesame Street" character Cookie Monster. When the child pushes a button on the front, Mr. Monster says, "Time to truck." But a Kmart manager in Lakewood, Colo., confirms "truck" doesn't sound all that clear. "It definitely comes out with an 'f'," she says. The foul-mouthed shirt came to the attention of Kmart after a complaint by angry parents who said their 19-month-old son picked up a "dirty word" from his T-shirt. (UPI) ...*Just a manufacturing error — the shirts were supposed to be size XL, not 3T.*

Fictional Character: Mofakharul Shahin bought a rat-infested building to convert into a new curry restaurant. He spent 100,000 pounds (US$170,000) cleaning it up, inside and out, but the Islington, England, city council thought little of his effort, thank you. It's now so clean it's "out of step with the neighbours," the council complains. "They want it to be dirty and scruffy like other buildings in the street. Can they be serious?" an exasperated Shahin complained. (Reuters) ...*We've been meaning to talk to you about the food. It's good, which puts it out of character for the whole country.*

A Mind is a Terrible Thing to Waste: Colorado Governor Roy Romer is under fire for the way he spent $2.9 million from a special energy conservation fund, money that was supposed to provide weather insulation for low-income housing. Instead, he issued an executive order that the money, a third of the fund's annual budget that had been slated to weatherize 1,523 homes, should instead be spent on Western Governors University, also known as "Internet University", an initiative being put together by 18 states to take higher education online. Each of the states was supposed to contribute $100,000. "There are a lot of good ideas that can be killed off because you're worrying, 'Is everybody paying the exact amount?'," Romer said after multiplying Colorado's contribution 29 times, adding he thinks using energy conservation funds for such a purpose is valid since the new university will have no buildings, thus students will not be driving to and from the college. "This is an innovative way to save energy," the governor claims. "Quite frankly, we need to be forward-thinking here." (Rocky Mountain News) ...*Indeed. Voters will be anxiously thinking forward to the next election.*

Pole Taxed: When the women's section of England's Bristol West Labour Party learned that one of its new members was in the process of a sex change, they voted to throw her out of the meeting. Rosalind Mitchell, who was elected to the Bristol City Council a year ago, still has not completed her gender reassignment surgery and, the group said, is thus still a man and therefore not welcome to attend their meetings. "My passport says I'm a woman," complained Mitchell afterward. "My driving licence says I'm a woman. My National Health Service records say I'm a woman." (AFP) ...*The headline: "Politician says Her Penis Lied about her Being a Man".*

Hillbilly Honeymoon: The Buckhannon-Upshur (W.Va.) Chamber of Commerce is sponsoring a wedding contest to lure people to move to the area. The winner, who must submit a 100-word-or-less essay saying why a wedding in the hills of West Virginia would be a "dream come true", will get a $15,000 package that includes blood tests, the ceremony, formal wear, an acre of land to live on, and a scholarship for the winner's first-born. (AP) ...*Not included: the wedding shotgun.*

Let Us Prey: Britain's Avon Silversmiths is launching a new vestment accessory at the annual National Christian Resources Exhibition: a crucifix with a built-in robbery alarm. "It looks like an ordinary crucifix, but one tug will set it off — and it's loud," a company spokesman says. The 169-pound (US$283) cross is the company's response to reports that one in three British clergy have been attacked on the job. But pastors in Kentucky have a better idea: they have succeeded in their quest to amend the state's concealed weapons law, which specifically excluded churches from the allowable locations citizens could carry weapons. Ministers and priests were upset by the exclusion and lobbied for the right to carry guns to fend off robbers after collection plates. An amendment to the law has passed to eliminate the loophole. (Reuters, 2) ...*The Lord helps those who help themselves; southern preachers shoot those who help themselves.*

Take a Flying Leap: Cook County (Ill.) Judge Michael Murphy is unhappy with Paul Iverson. Neighbors complained that the Arlington Heights man had too much junk in his yard. Despite removing "30 truckloads" of junk, the judge says it's not enough and is fining the man $500 a day until he complies with the court's order. The fine so far: $49,000, and the judge hints jail may be next. Judge Murphy was not amused by one attempt Iverson made to keep from having to move the fuselage of an old 727 airliner out of his yard. Iverson got license plates for the airplane and says the plane is a "recreational vehicle". (UPI) ...*Only for Illinoisans named Hugh Hefner.*

Chopper Stopper
Swedish Dentist Seizes Teeth in Payment Dispute
AFP headline

Scarlet Letter: Delaware has just passed a new law requiring sex offenders to get a special mark on their driver's licenses. People convicted of sex offenses will get a "Y" designation on the front of their license upon release from prison. On the back, in the area where it shows regular driving restrictions, such as the need to wear glasses, will be a fuller explanation. (AP) ...*Remember, kids: before accepting a ride from a stranger, be sure to ask to see his license first.*

Politics as Usual: Alberto Russi's wife is glad he was convicted — maybe now he'll stop meddling in politics, she says. "But I love politics," Russi, 92, retorted after he pleaded no contest to four counts of voter fraud for tampering with absentee ballots in the recent Miami, Fla., mayoral election. Sentencing guidelines called for a one-year jail term but the judge, citing Russi's age, instead sentenced him to two years of probation. (UPI) ...*He may actually have preferred jail — it would have been a good way to spend a year with well-known politicians.*

Fighting Words: "I was wrong. I should not have said what I said," Jane Fonda admits. "My comments were inaccurate." She was backing off from a speech she made to the United Nations Population Fund agency where she said, "In the northern part of Georgia, children are starving to death. People live in tar-paper shacks with no indoor plumbing, and so forth." Georgia Gov. Zell Miller, a native of the northern part of the state, was outraged. "Maybe the view from your penthouse apartment is not as clear as it needs to be," he told Fonda, referring to her living area on top of the CNN Tower in Atlanta, Ga. (AP) ...*Hey, cut her some slack. Maybe she was having flashbacks from her days in North Vietnam.*

Don't Do It: Now that everyone knows smoking is dangerous, the U.S. Surgeon General is turning his attention to other pressing health problems. Dr. David Satcher says a new surgeon general's report will argue that the country needs to pay more attention to suicide. "It is hard for many to believe that more people in this country die from suicide than homicide, but it is true," he proclaimed at a meeting of the American Society of Suicidology. The report is due in about a year and will include recommendations on how to improve suicide awareness. (Reuters) ...*Surgeon General's Warning: Suicide may be dangerous to your health.*

Dream On: When Jimmy Carter was president of the U.S., Eleanor Mondale, daughter of the vice president, said she had a problem one night while sleeping in the vice president's mansion. "I was so scared, I fainted," she writes in Swing magazine. "Upon coming to, I reached for the phone and picked up the 'hot line' to the Secret Service Command Post. I whispered that there was a man in my room and hung up. Minutes later, two agents busted into the room, guns drawn." There was no man in the room: she told the bodyguards she had seen a ghost. Secret Service agents "requested that I NEVER DO THAT AGAIN!" (AP) ...*She wasn't the first, or last, Democrat haunted by Casper Weinberger.*

Edur Woh: "We often have to seek help from the German or French language departments of Victoria University to clarify the meaning or pronunciation of names," notes a spokesman for a New Zealand horse racing association. But the language experts didn't help when it came to Tulsy Tsan, a filly entered to race in Wellington. The name wasn't German or French, it was English — spelled backwards. When the name's etiology was discovered, she was pulled from the race, but was allowed to re-enter after being renamed "Ben Again". (Reuters) ...*After "Ben Dover" was rejected too.*

There and Back: The road to Hell needs work. "It'll close the whole town," complains Hell Chamber of Commerce President Jim Ley. "That's where our money comes from. It'll kill us." A bridge on the main road that leads to Hell, Mich., is in bad shape and the repair crew needs three months to fix it. "It's probably going to put a couple of us out of business," one shop owner conceded. (AP) ...*They shouldn't worry: the road crew's intentions are good.*

Rageous Interruptus: In an attempt to reduce "road rage", police in Ontario, Canada, are pulling over drivers that look angry to give them a survey, asking 10 questions about driving habits. "When you get a situation where one or two people are road raging, they'll tell us why they got in that state of mind," claims Provincial Police Sergeant Peggy Gamble. (Reuters) ...*While others just scream, "You made me late to work for this?"*

Man's Best Friend: When an elderly couple's dog fell into a ventilation shaft, someone was there to help them. The Budapest, Hungary, couple watched as a man identified only as Jozsef P. came to their aid by lowering himself down the 20-meter shaft on a rope. The man then tied the rope to the dog so they could pull the animal to safety. The relieved couple hurried off with the dog but, Jozsef says, they didn't bother to throw the rope back down to him. A passerby heard his dwindling calls for help — four days later. He is hospitalized in serious condition suffering from malnutrition and dehydration. (AFP) ... *"Maybe the only thing worse than having to give gratitude ...is having to accept it." —William Faulkner (1897–1962), U.S. novelist.*

But to Be Sure, They'll Check Back Later

Study Links Menopause, Aging
AP headline

Hand Canceled: Police in Channelview, Texas, say John Edwin May, already on parole after an aggravated robbery conviction, tried to rob the local post office. They allege he handed a clerk a note saying he had explosives and wanted money. The clerk took the note to her supervisor, who then led all the employees out the back door. "Before [May] knew it, he was standing there all alone," a sheriff spokesman said. May was arrested "without incident". No explosives were found. (Houston Chronicle) ...*But* *it may lead to a new "Priority Mailbomb" service: three sticks of dynamite sent anywhere in three days for just three bucks.*

Please Form a Single Line: Convicted drunk drivers in Reno, Nev., were ordered to attend a Victim Impact Panel to listen to people talk about family members killed by drunk drivers. Police watched as 14 of the court-ordered attendees drove up in their cars. All 14 were arrested and face additional sentences of six months in jail and a $1,000 fine — their driving licenses had been suspended as part of their convictions. (AP) ...*The only surprising thing is that none of them were arrested for drunk driving.*

He's Not Bad, He's Just Drawn That Way: Toronto, Ont., Canada, police are looking for Homer Simpson. Sort of. A man that has robbed three Toronto banks in the last several months has been dubbed the Homer Simpson Bandit because of his "striking resemblance" to the character on "The Simpsons" animated TV series. "It's the way he looks and the way he holds himself up," a police spokesman said of the resemblance. (Victoria B.C. Times Colonist) ...*If he goes into banks and only manages to hold himself up, he really is a lot like Homer Simpson.*

Bad Boy II: Brian James Diaz, 21, has been arrested after a bank robbery in Detroit, Mich. Police say that Diaz convinced a 12-year-old boy to pull off the heist after promising to split the money with him. The robbery went awry when the boy dropped the money bag after a dye packet slipped in with the money exploded as he ran out the door. Diaz, police say, not wanting to end up with nothing, then tried to turn the boy in and claim a reward offered for the robber's capture. The boy was not charged. (AP) ...*But he will have to stand in the corner of the bank lobby with a dunce cap.*

And You Can Quote Me: A Canadian legislator has been revealed as the author of several letters published in a local newspaper saying what a great politician he is. Liberal Party member of the provincial legislature Paul Reitsma of Vancouver Island, B.C., admitted writing the letters after the suspicious newspaper hired a handwriting analyst. In at least 10 letters signed with false names, Reitsma praised himself and panned rivals — and once managed to misspell his own name and the word "hypocrisy". One letter accused a rival of being "politically dishonest". Reitsma refuses to resign, but admits he is "ashamed and humiliated." (Reuters) ...*Although he didn't sign his own name to the confession.*

Playboy Bunny Slope: Crested Butte Mountain resort is rethinking its traditional end-of-season ritual. The Colorado ski resort has hosted nude skiers celebrating the last day on the slopes, but it's getting out of hand, the resort says. This year, "hundreds" of skiers doffed their ski suits for naked runs down the slope. "Our mountain is a family mountain," resort spokeswoman Gina Kroft said. Hundreds of bare skiers instead of mere dozens "just doesn't have that light, fun feeling anymore." Kroft says the resort may not ban nude skiing altogether, but they'll try to come up with a new ritual before next year's closing. (UPI) ...*Herding celebrity skiers into trees has already been rejected, thank you.*

A Modest Proposal: The city of Carbondale, Colo., doesn't want residents to spray their weeds with herbicides. But they don't want weeds growing around town, either. So the city is suggesting an alternative: it's urging citizens to eat the weeds. John Phillip, a member of the city's Environmental Board, says dandelions suffer from a poor image. "It's really a vegetable," he says. "It's only a weed in the eyes of people who grew up in the '50s and '60s and moved to the suburbs." (AP) ...*Now, about the sewage problem....*

Checkout: The British Library is celebrating the opening of their new building in central London. However, the library was horrified when it was pointed out that there was a typo in a huge promotional banner hanging on the side of the structure: "The British Library. For the nation's written heritage [*sic*]". The AFP wire service gleefully pointed out the gaffe in a story headlined, "British Library Embarassed [*sic*] by Mispelling [*sic*] its Heritage". (AFP) ...*People who live in glass houses should not throw stones.*

Coincidence? You be the Judge

Koko the Gorilla Chats on Internet
AP

Consumers Get Health Advice on Net
AP, later the same day

Chicken: David Flannery Jr., 22, and a friend were walking along railroad tracks near Berkeley Springs, W.Va., when a train approached. The two men "competed" to see which would stand the longest on the tracks in front of the oncoming train. The unidentified friend jumped "just in time," a sheriff deputy said, but Flannery was hit and thrown 70 feet by the impact. He is hospitalized in serious condition. (AP) ...*Your task: decide which man won.*

I Came, I Sawed, I Studied: Researchers at the University of Erlangen-Nurnberg, Germany, have found that students who snore while they sleep averaged 64 on school exams, while non-snorers averaged 70. Worse, the snoring students are twice as likely to fail the exams completely. Thus, the researchers concluded, snorers are more likely to be poorer students than those who sleep quietly. (UPI) ...*Especially if they do it in class.*

Studious Sleeper II: Police in Reston, Va., have broken up a prostitution operation run by a 13-year-old boy who told police he was known as "Mr. Pimp". The boy managed to talk a number of 12- and 13-year-old girls, all fellow students at Langston Hughes Middle School, into paying him to be part of his "sex club". He then solicited male classmates to have sex with as many as three of the girls at once, though police don't think any sexual encounters actually took place before they busted the ring. The boy has been sentenced to 60 days in juvenile detention and up to six months of counseling. (AP) ...*That kid has a long, successful career in telephone sales ahead of him.*

McCourtfight: The McDonald's restaurant chain has lost a trademark fight in Austria against a hair-styling chain called McHair. "Of course we are not happy about it," a spokesman from the hamburger joint commented. "'Mc' is the world-famous part of McDonald's brandname and is used for other products like McChicken or particular services such as McDrive." However, the food giant does not plan to appeal the decision. (AFP) *...McDrive? Just what we need: a drive-through driving school.*

Clogged Artery: A tanker truck carrying warm animal fat to a processing plant to be made into fabric softener overturned in Cincinnati, Ohio, during rush hour traffic, spilling 6,700 gallons of fat on Interstate 74. Road crews closed the highway for three days while trying to figure out how to clear away the slick fat — sand, high-pressure water and solvents didn't work since the grease had oozed into cracks and the grooved pavement, then cooled and congealed. So Proctor & Gamble, which is based in Cincinnati, donated 3.5 tons of "Dawn" dishwashing detergent, which is advertised with the slogan "Dawn takes grease out of your way." It worked. "This is, by far, the most extreme case of grease we've dealt with," a P&G spokesman said. "We're delighted it worked." (AP) *...Most extreme case of grease they've dealt with? Obviously, then, P&G doesn't have the McDonald's contract.*

Croaked: Thomas Capriola, 28, of New York is free on bail after being charged with selling video tapes of women in high heels stomping on frogs and rodents. The tapes were a "foot-fetish type of thing," said Adam Gross of the Suffolk County Society for the Prevention of Cruelty to Animals. They had such titles as "Vanessa's Frog Stomp", "Debby the Destructor" and "Vanessa, Topless Crusher". Capriola faces "possibly thousands of counts" of animal cruelty, each of which is punishable by a $1,000 fine and a year in jail. Police found mice and several pair of high-heeled shoes in a raid on his home. They are still searching for the women who did the stomping. (Reuters) *...They might save themselves some trouble: see if the shoes fit Capriola.*

Rising Expectations: Former U.S. Sen. Bob Dole, who ran against Bill Clinton for president, announced on CNN's "Larry King

Live" show that he was a test subject for the anti-impotence drug, Viagra. "It is a great drug," enthused the retired senator, who previously had urged men to get prostate checkups after he was diagnosed with prostate cancer. The next day, Dole's wife Libby was asked about the drug. "Let me just say ... it's a great drug. OK?" (AP, 2) ...*Mrs. Clinton, on the other hand, is asking Pfizer if they can develop a new drug, AntiViagra.*

Grave Expectations: Donal Bredin-Smith, 65, a chiropodist in County Clare, Ireland, bought a double burial plot for himself and his wife, but now they're divorced. So he took out an advertisement in the local paper looking for someone to share the grave: "Spacious room for two occupants. Present owner seeks one female gravemate. First one in takes bottom berth. Garlic eaters and smokers need not apply." He has received at least 23 replies so far. "Five of the Irish women who rang wanted to have a pre-grave relationship, and I might take one of them up on it," Bredin-Smith says. (AFP) ...*Bringing new meaning to the age-old dating question, "Where'd you dig that one up?"*

Special Delivery: A parking meter officer in Tampa, Fla., stopped at a black BMW that was parked at an expired meter. The officer noticed several things: the car already had a ticket on the windshield, the car was only a block from police headquarters, and there was a man on the seat, tied hand and foot, and shot several times in the head. Robert Enlow, 69, was rushed to a hospital, but it was too late: he died a short time later. Enlow was to be a witness in a federal fraud trial. (Reuters) ...*Tampa detectives, no doubt, will rule it a suicide.*

With a Few More Years of Careful Teutonic Engineering, it May be Able to Move Backward, Too

German Magnetic Train Moves Forward

AP headline

Boss! Da Plane! U.S. Customs agents were following a suspected drug-smuggling airplane that had crossed the border into Texas from Mexico. They followed it, and followed it, all the way to Michigan, where the pilot ran out of fuel. Customs agents watched from above as the plane crash-landed into a baseball field behind Noble Middle School in Detroit, killing the pilot. They also watched several people near the school who witnessed the crash as they ran up to the plane, grabbed bags of cash and marijuana, and ran. (Reuters) *...Otherwise known as the "Ganja from Heaven" case.*

Now We Know: What happens when the *...uh...* excrement hits the fan? Subasinghe Premasiri was in court in Sri Lanka on theft charges. He smuggled in feces in a plastic bag and threw them at a police officer. He missed. Instead, the hurled hunks hit a spinning ceiling fan, splattering everyone in the Colombo magistrate court. He pleaded guilty to contempt and received an eight-month sentence. (AFP) *...Otherwise known as the "CaCa from Heaven" case.*

The Antti-Christ: Lutherans in Finland are upset. But they're not sure if they're more upset at two Lutheran priests, or at the church's refusal to punish them. The Rev. Olli Arola has publically declared that Jesus might have been married to Mary Magdalene, and also said he doubted the immaculate conception. Meanwhile, the Rev. Antti Kylliainen has published a book declaring that Hell does not exist, and that everyone will get into Heaven. The church refuses to fire either minister. "Priests also have the right of free speech and personal opinions," declared Helsinki Bishop Eero Huovinen. (Reuters) *...Finally, a church smart enough to know the difference between heresy and hearsay.*

Flipper: Kevin Morrison, 16, of Rockford, Ill., was on a diving trip off the Florida Keys with his family when a tiger shark swam by. The boy reached out and yanked its tail. Big mistake: the startled shark turned around and bit him in the chest. Apparently, however, a 16-year-old boy is too big a bite to chew for a 3-foot tiger shark: it couldn't let go of the lad's chest. It held on all the way to the hospital, where doctors removed it surgically. Morrison was released from the hospital the same day. (AP) ...*It's not nice to fool Mother Nature.*

Amway Hits the Highway: The Chinese government is nervous over direct-sales companies after at least one fly-by-night scheme collapsed after collecting $170 each from thousands of "peasants", the government says. So now they're cracking down on giant direct companies such as Amway, Avon and Mary Kay by banning door-to-door sales. The problem isn't just with the sales methods: local newspapers say the companies promote "weird cults" and "excessive hugging". (Newsweek) ...*Apparently, it's rude in communist countries for people to grab each other and jump up and down crying, "We're rich! We're rich!"*

Marriage Encounter: Michael and Bonnie Martin of Fresno, Calif., were getting marriage counseling at their church. Michael arrived late, drinking a beer, so Bonnie decided to walk out. That, police say, is when Michael pulled out a gun and started shooting at her. Wounded, Bonnie reached into her purse and pulled out her own gun to shoot back. The battle continued into the parking lot of St. James Episcopal Cathedral. "It's a good thing that he had been drinking because he could have hit her more," said the Rev. Bud Searcy. "He was a lousy shot." Still, Bonnie is hospitalized in serious condition. Michael was treated for a superficial wound and has been charged with attempted murder. Prosecutors have declined to levy charges against Mrs. Martin. (AP) ...*That's not what the pastor meant when he said "Let's see if we can troubleshoot this problem, Michael."*

Look Out Below: Daredevil biker Evel Knievel's record of jumping his motorcycle over 19 cars has been broken. Bubba Blackwell successfully jumped 20 cars in Everett, Mass., beating his own record of 14 cars. He was going so fast during the stunt he also nearly jumped over his landing ramp. Will he try to best the 20-car jump? "I don't know," Blackwell said, adding he wasn't sure just how much clearance he had because "I had my eyes closed." (UPI) ...*Thereby disproving the notion that he's a complete idiot.*

There's a Sucker Born Every Millennium: Britain's Royal Geographical Society says the first sunup of the new millennium will fall on Pitt Island, off New Zealand. So the Millennium Adventure Company has purchased exclusive rights to film the sunup on the first day of the new era. But a rival company, New Dawn 2000, says it also purchased exclusive rights to film the dawn from there. The two London-based companies are now squabbling over an island hillside, with one threatening to build a fence to block the other's view. Meanwhile, Tonga says it's the closest country to the new dawn, but a Tongan magazine says "Tonga's casual 'wait and see us dancing and singing and we'll charge you' approach might fail to exploit this once in a millennium opportunity for global television coverage." (AFP) ...*Like anyone is going to get up in the morning to look at the sun after partying all night.*

Someone's Not Doing it Right
Study: Sex differs in U.S., Europe
UPI headline

Guilty Until Proven Innocent: Two U.S. congressmen were targeted by a "rogue" Internal Revenue Service agent while they were in office, they say. The agent fabricated charges of bribery and money laundering against Senate majority leader Howard Baker Jr. in 1989. Ex-Rep. James Quillen testified that the IRS agent would go into bars and loudly announce, "We're going to get that crook, Congressman Quillen!" The IRS ignored evidence that the agent was an alcoholic and out of control, and instead tried to discredit the agents who turned him in, forcing one of them to go on raids without a weapon or bulletproof vest. The rogue agent continued to work for the IRS until he was arrested for cocaine possession. No credible evidence was found against either politician, and the investigations were dropped. (UPI) ...*In other words, powerful politicians get preferential treatment from the IRS.*

A Boy Named Sue: Attorney Larry Klayman wants to stop government corruption. His chief tool? Lawsuits — he's filed 17 cases against the Clinton administration alone. In fact, the founder of "Judicial Watch" is so adept at filing lawsuits that he sued his mother for $40,000 in a dispute over the care of his grandmother. "It's painful, but I'm not going to child bash," said his mother, Shirley Feinberg. Brother Steven Klayman is even less forthcoming: he declined comment, explaining "I don't want to be sued." (Newsweek) ...*Mom's just glad she talked him out of working for the IRS.*

Everybody Loves a Woman in Uniform: Firefighter Caroline Paul doesn't mind being mistaken for her twin sister, Alexandra, an actress who plays a lifeguard on the TV show "Baywatch", known for featuring shapely actresses in red lifeguard bathing suits. "I could be coming off a fire truck and someone will say, 'Hey, you're that girl from that Baywatch show. The one with the real breasts'," Caroline says. But she has not been bitten by the acting bug. "If there's a fire, I want to be there," she said. "Maybe because in being so close to death, I think I understand what it means to be truly alive." (AP) ...*Firefighters are always in heat.*

Thirty-Two-Cent Solution: The U.S. Postal Service is having trouble in El Camino Village, a rough neighborhood in Los Angeles, Calif. Gang members beat up a mailman, so another carrier was assigned to the route. He felt so threatened by the gangbangers' threats he put in for a transfer. After four days of no mail deliveries, service has been resumed — with a third carrier getting an escort by sheriff deputies. (UPI) ...*Neither rain nor sleet, snow nor the hail of bullets will keep them from their appointed rounds.*

Hard Sell: Mrs. Banks said no. Repeatedly. But vacuum cleaner salesman Ricardo Vasquez wouldn't take no for an answer, Mrs. Banks says. Vasquez thought she might change her mind, and kept pressing her. That's when her husband, Fred, decided enough was enough. Police say Mr. Banks chased Vasquez out of his West Haven, Conn., house with a .22-caliber pistol. Both men were arrested, with Vasquez charged with criminal trespass and soliciting without a permit, and Banks charged with breach of peace. (AP) ...*If nothing else, Vasquez now has a chance to change Banks' mind while they sit in their cell together.*

Name Game: The city of Saratoga, Calif., insists its town name does not mean "floating scum on the water", as some have said the Mohawk Indian name translates. The town, near San Jose, is proposing a new translation instead: "Hillside Country of the Great River, Place of the Swift Water". (Reuters) ...*More accurately, "Town Not Allowed to be Part of Silicon Valley, Grasping at Straws".*

Name Defame: Calling someone a bitch is not defamation of character, Manhattan Supreme Court Justice Herman Cahn has ruled. Cahn dismissed a $50,000 lawsuit by Gay Culverhouse, 50, who objected to her boss applying the word to her, noting that other courts have held that there can be no "objective proof" whether or not the term applies to someone. (UPI) ...*Defamation of character, no. Definition of character, perhaps.*

Clothes Unmake the Man: The 29-year-old mayor of Chepstow, Wales, has quit rather than dress up for city council meetings. Armand Watts, 29, a hairdresser, liked to wear T-shirts and jeans. "I really don't see the point of wearing a suit, shirt and tie to sit around in council meetings," Watts says. "Although the meetings are public they are so boring that no one else attends." Pam Burchill, a retired nurse that led the fight for a council dress code, admits she is "old fashioned", but "I believe that if we are elected we have a duty to maintain high standards and that includes a dress code." She is now the new mayor of Chepstow. (AFP) ... *You can't fight city hall.*

Crime Rate Going Up: A shipment of the hot-selling anti-impotence drug Viagra was stolen at the port of La Guaira, Venezuela. The pills, which normally sell for about $10 each in the U.S., will probably fetch about $17 each on the black market, officials said. (AP) ...*Police say they are looking for a band of hardened criminals.*

Surely to be Appealed

Judge Says Texas is Part of U.S.

AP headline

Vocational Training: A 16-year-old boy who drove his car around a railroad crossing barrier crashed into the side of a passing train, police say. San Mateo, Calif., rescue crews had to cut Jesse Jones from the mangled wreck of his mother's Pontiac, but the boy escaped with minor injuries. Meanwhile, officials in Lafayette, Ind., credit a train conductor for saving the life of a little girl who was lying on the railroad tracks as his train approached at 24 mph. Knowing he could not jump off the train and outrun it in time to save the 19-month-old girl, conductor Robert Mohr climbed onto a railing on front of the locomotive and kicked her from the path of the oncoming train. Area officials call Mohr a hero, but he shrugs it off. "I did what anybody would have done," he said. (San Francisco Chronicle, AP) *...It isn't doing it that's heroic, it's thinking — in time — of what to do in the first place.*

Vocational Training II: Heath Hess, 24, needed to make a phone call. As he walked through Hornell, N.Y., talking on his cellular phone, he drowned out road noise by sticking his finger in his opposite ear. One of the noises that he thus didn't hear: the whistle of a freight train approaching from behind him — Hess was walking on railroad tracks. The engineer on the train "tried everything" to get Hess' attention. When blowing the whistle didn't work, the engineer "climbed out of the front of the engine and threw a water bottle at him," a police spokesman said. "Unfortunately, the water bottle missed and the train didn't." Hess was treated for minor injuries. (AP) *...To heck with Hess: what did the person he was talking to think was going on?*

Hi Ho, Hi Ho, It's Off to Court We Go: Happy Stewart, 16, admitted to assault and violence charges in Falkirk Sheriff Court in Scotland. She said she flew off the handle because she was "fed up" with her given name. The court ordered her to attend an anger management course. Stewart said she plans to change her first name to Elizabeth. (AFP) ...*Maybe "Grumpy" would be more fitting.*

Looking for a Few Good Men: Sharon Garmize was a bit surprised when a letter addressed to Sam Garmize arrived at her home. It was from the U.S. Selective Service agency, demanding that Sam register for the military draft. Sam is a blue crown mealy Amazon parrot. "Sometimes we get a dog. Sometimes we get a cat," said a Selective Service spokesman, noting that lists of 18-year-olds are purchased from private vendors. "This time we got a parrot." (AP) ...*Bird brain you say? He could make General!*

Show Me the Money! When rioters approached Bank Bali in western Jakarta, Indonesia, bank employees were sure their fate would be the same as other banks in the area: looting and fire-bombs. With few security guards to rely on, the bank employees got an idea: they threw 10,000, 20,000 and 50,000 rupiah (US$1, 2 and 5) notes into the unruly crowd to distract them from looting. (AFP) ...*Otherwise known as the "Throw the baby out with the bath water" tactic.*

Give Me the Money! "There's no crime going on here," said congressional candidate Hale McGee during a television appearance, insisting his Ontario, Calif., district does not have a crime problem. A short time later, McGee and his campaign manager were robbed at gunpoint after stopping at a gas station. "I feel like I have egg and goo all over me," a sheepish McGee told reporters afterward. (AP) ...*Don't worry, Hale: it's natural to mess yourself in a situation like that.*

An Apple a Day: Researchers at Nestec, the research and development laboratory for the Swiss chocolate manufacturer Nestlé, say chocolate may hold the key to curing cancer. "Cocoa is conceivably a treasure chest of compounds with potentially beneficial effects on human health," claims Nicholas Jardine. "In the early steps towards cancer, things found in cocoa have been found to have beneficial effects, usually in test tube experiments, but occasionally in the body," he said. "Who knows, maybe in 20 years time chocolate bars will be required eating in school lunch boxes for their protective health properties." (Reuters) ...*Leaving* *kids cancer-free, but toothless obese cardiac patients who can't sleep at night.*

Add Saltpeter to Taste: Madison, Wis., police chief Richard Williams turned his oven to 350 degrees, popped in some turkey, and laid down to rest while it cooked. "Shortly thereafter, BOOM!" his spokeswoman said later. The boom was a gunshot — the chief forgot that he had hidden his service revolver in the oven, one of several strange places he hides his gun to keep it out of the hands of burglars. No one was injured in the incident, but the chief suggested to the mayor that he be given a one-day suspension without pay for violating the department's gun safety policy. (AP) *...Just a few more spices and he'll have a sure-fire recipe.*

A Picture is Worth 1,000 Words: Photographs of murder scenes and car wrecks grace the walls. A dead, stuffed dog. Such are the items on display at the The Museum of Death in San Diego, Calif. "I'm about to lose my dinner," said one visitor, who insisted she was dragged into the exhibit by a friend. "There's a reason that the general public does not see this stuff in the paper." The dead dog is "the most profound piece we have," says Cathee Shultz, who owns the museum with her husband, J.D. Healy. "People get so upset about a dead dog." Then there's the stained T-shirt worn by a man who was executed in the electric chair. "This is how we try to educate people," Healy said. "We educate through shock." (AP) *...Funny: that's just what the executioner said about the condemned prisoner.*

Kansas Woman Related to Blessed Virgin: Margarita Holguin Cazares says a plaque of the Virgin Mary she has at her house in Lewis, Kan., weeps blood. The local Diocese, skeptical of such supposed miracles, had the blood tested. It is in fact blood — and its DNA matches Mrs. Cazares' blood. But the test results haven't changed the mind of true believers, who still think the phenomenon is a miracle. "If they are insinuating that Maggie is putting the blood on the plaque, how do you explain it when she's not even near it?" asks Cathy Woolard, the editor of the local newspaper. Woolard says maybe the matching DNA is part of the miracle. "With God, anything's possible — who are we to question?" (AP) ...*If it's not good enough for the Diocese, it's not good enough for me.*

Your Tax Dollars at Work

Legislature Follows the Law, Does Little

UPI headline

Exploding Idiocy Syndrome: Consumers need to be aware that not everything on the Internet is true, says Canadian medical librarian Susan M. Murray of the Toronto (Ont.) Reference Library. Many online medical sites, she says, contain suspect information. "This poor woman who called us was frantic, she thought she had exploding head syndrome," Murray says. The woman had learned of the "syndrome" on a web site and assumed the malady was real. The site was a hoax. "This is a perfect example of people jumping on the Internet and believing everything." (AP) ...*Caveat surfor.*

Step Right Up: In order to attract customers, a new chain of bars along Spain's Catalonian coast plans to offer something extra with each 1,000-peseta (US$7) drink: a French kiss. Each bar will have four waitresses and one waiter on staff to provide the service, though the staff may refuse to administer the liplock "if the client is not in good condition," manager Eduardo Esteban says. Further, customers will be handcuffed first "make sure their hands do not wander." (AFP) ...*Nice touch: in most places, the handcuffs would be extra.*

Sock it to Me: Two men in Southport, Merseyside, England, who told people they needed to collect used socks for charity, managed to collect 10,000 pairs. But the two, Steven Bain, 27, and Steven Gawthrop, 31, were actually foot fetishists, police say, and the socks were piled all over their apartment up to 18 inches deep. "They were all over the furniture, hanging from lampshades and even in the microwave, frying pan and cooker," said one officer who raided the flat. "It was like there had been an explosion in a sock factory." Police also found pictures of some of the victims holding up their socks before donating them. The pictured included two uniformed policemen and a traffic warden. (Times of London) *...However, police were unable to find any two that matched.*

Up, Up and Away: Roberta Burke, 61, says that when her longtime boyfriend Francis Bernardo, 70, took the anti-impotence drug Viagra, they had sex for the first time in four years — and then he left her for another woman. She is now suing for $2 million, saying the drug broke up their 10-year relationship. Bernardo's lawyer, Raoul Felder, says Burke is just after the man's money and is using Viagra as a scapegoat. "Have you ever heard of an inanimate object breaking up your marriage? You might as well name a chair," he said. (AP) *...That would depend on how the chair was advertised.*

Swell Idea: The Church of England has announced it is very happy with Viagra. It isn't necessarily the action of the drug they like; rather, they have stock in its manufacturer, Pfizer, which has nearly doubled in less than a year. "We certainly have had a good return on that investment," a spokesman for the church commissioners said. The church owns about two million pounds (US$3.2 million) worth of the stock. (Reuters) *...Truly a wonder drug: it even works on money.*

Bull! The Nevada Department of Transportation has vetoed the plans of the town of Mesquite for a "running of the bulls", patterned after the running in Pamplona, Spain, to help bring in tourists. "The applicants had indicated that 12 bulls would chase 1,000 people through the main road of Mesquite in front of 5,000 spectators," said a DOT spokesman. "It's our decision that a state highway should not be used for a risky event such as this." (AP) *...Perhaps a more American version: 1,000 snorting voters chasing 100 politicians in front of a cheering TV audience of millions.*

Fancy Geomancy: Villagers in Qiongshan, in China's Guangdong province, were not happy with the layout of a bridge into town. It had bad *feng shui,* they said, indicating the "energy flow" through the bridge was unlucky for the village and bringing bad

fortune. They solved the problem by blowing the bridge up. (AFP)
...Wouldn't it have been cheaper to hang a mirror on one end?

Don't Bees: Police in Sacramento, Calif., solved a string of rob-
beries by the so-called "Romper Room Gang" after the robbers
allegedly used some of the $1.5 million of robbery proceeds to
start a recording company. The gang was caught after releasing
the album "The Rompalation". The album's lyrics described a
robbery very much like one that police were investigating. So far,
27 people have been charged in the holdups, and one has been
convicted. (Reuters) *...Wherever you are, whatever you're doing,
Miss Nancy can see you in her Magic Mirror.*

What He Said: President Bill Clinton has ordered that starting
October 1, federal documents be written in plain English, not
bureaucratic gobbledygook that confuses people. "By using plain
language, we send a clear message about what the government is
doing, what it requires and what services it offers," Clinton wrote
in the order. "Short is better than long. Active is better than
passive," agreed Vice President Al Gore. "Clarity helps advance
understanding." (AP) *...This consequential quasi-governmental
commandment, corroborated by the plenipotentiary, dictates an
innovational manifesto which will decidedly actuate a diminution
in obfuscation.*

Bountiful Bunco: John Santner, 33, pleaded guilty to fraud and
drug charges, ending his career as "the city's most prolific bunco
artist ever," said a spokesman for the San Francisco, Calif., police.
Santner managed to steal more than $4 million over two years,
investigators say, by writing bad checks, or using forged driver's
licenses to cash stolen checks. Police recovered $1.5 million
worth of stolen checks that had not yet been cashed, as well as
780 $100 bills. Santner "ran this like any legitimate business,"
said Assistant District Attorney Bob Ring. "It's not your typical
poo-butt who walks into a bank with a bogus check." (San
Francisco Chronicle) *...If the D.A. wants cops to identify with him,
he really needs to work on his "street talk."*

Generation X Can Wait

Baby Boomers Not
Planning to Retire

UPI headline

What's in a Name? Darion Northrup "Sam" Castle, 63, has been hiding from authorities for 21 years. Castle, convicted of fraud in the death of his girlfriend in 1970, lost an appeal and was ordered to prison. He never showed up. Authorities finally found him living in Seattle, Wash., under the name Mark Bradfield — the name of his prosecutor in the fraud case. (UPI) ...*Imitation is the sincerest form of flattery.*

Mile High Airlines: South African Airways is asking police to charge two of its passengers with public indecency, the airline announced. A couple on a flight from London to Johannesburg was not concerned with who saw what they were doing, the airline says. "It was the most callous display of lust I have ever seen," said one. "I could understand it if they covered themselves with a blanket, but no: it was wham, bam, right there in the seat, in the missionary position," her husband confirmed. The couple only stopped when the captain stepped into the passenger cabin and told them that his airplane was "not a shag house". (Reuters) ...*Unless, of course, they pay full first class fares.*

Million Mile High Club: With hopes of sending astronauts on a mission to Mars, which will take about three years, NASA is finally coming to grips with the possibility that ...*gasp!*... a mixed crew of astronauts might, perhaps, someday, maybe, engage in space sex. However, a veteran Russian cosmonaut urges NASA to assign a crew without women to remove the temptation. "A young guy could hold out three years without women, then when he got back to Earth all women would love him," Musa Manarov, who has spent a total of a year and a half in space, claims. He adds it's easier to go without women in space than on Earth. "On Earth you see advertisements, television, someone going by. You'd go out of your mind, say, two years without women." But having a woman on a space mission would make such self-control impossible, he says. "It's like a weapon that could misfire. But if you didn't have the weapon at all it just won't go off." (Reuters) *...NASA is realistic enough to know the astronauts' weapons will be going off whether women are there or not.*

Operation Salad Dressing: Researchers at the Pacific Northwest National Laboratory in Richland, Wash., looking for a safe way to destroy more than 500,000 tons of surplus military explosives, think they may have found the solution: spinach. The "good-for-you" veggie contains an enzyme, nitroeductase, which, when mixed with water and a buffer solution, has the ability to safely "eat" explosives such as TNT. The Department of Defense is providing $1 million to study the "environmentally benign digestion process", which should take about three years. (UPI) *...There goes the military wasting time and money again. Popeye showed that spinach could neutralize high explosives decades ago.*

Vetoed: An "ordained exorcist" has attempted to chase the "dragons and serpents" from the U.S. Capitol. However, despite his efforts, which were aided by a Bible and a large silver cross, Baron Deacon says he failed to rid the building of its evil spirits. (AP) *...Exorcists are no match for demons with large reelection campaign budgets.*

How Are They Hanging? The Kingdom of Swaziland has not executed a prisoner since 1984, but it now has eight convicts on death row. Unfortunately, they no longer have a hangman. "We used to use a rotational hangman that we shared with Botswana and Lesotho, but now we want to have our own," says Minister of Justice Maweni Simelane. When they advertised that the position was open, the Ministry got applications from several countries. "A couple of weeks ago, two local women came to see me on this issue," the minister added. A rigorous interview process will screen the applicants. "If they face problems with their conscience, we'll find ourselves looking for another candidate," he said, though he refused to say what salary would be paid. (Reuters) *...Just doing a good job is ample reward.*

Just When You Thought it was Safe to Go Back in the Water: When two fishermen from Puglia, Italy, found a hand grenade, they didn't turn it over to authorities, they took it fishing. And when they saw some bubbles coming from the deep, they tossed the grenade in the water "hoping to stun fish". The bubbles weren't coming from fish, but from Teodoro Zuccaro's scuba tank. The blast killed the 43-year-old diver. The two fishermen have been charged with manslaughter, detonating an explosive, and poaching. (AP) ...*Of course poaching: divers aren't in season yet.*

Can't Trust Anyone Anymore: The National Partnership for Women & Families says that TV shows do not accurately reflect actual society. "It's a pretty distorted reflection," says spokeswoman Lauren Asher. "There are very few working moms on TV compared with the real world. Almost nobody's over 50, most adults are men, and child-care and elder-care just don't seem to come up." (UPI) ...*TV shows also consistently under-represent politicians, over-represent criminals, and do not reflect society's actual number of people with hemorrhoids, cancer, and acne, either.*

Chance of Conviction Estimated at 7 in 10
Russia's Statistics Boss Accused of Fraud
AFP headline

It Looks Like Rain: The city of Orlando, Fla., had better watch out, says preacher Pat Robertson. He says the city's tolerance of homosexuals and recognizing "Gay Pride Month" with banners in the streets will bring the wrath of God on them, in the form of earthquakes, meteors, or bad weather. "I would warn Orlando that you're right in the way of some serious hurricanes and I don't think I'd be waving those flags in God's face if I were you," Robertson lectured on his radio show. Most residents shrugged the warning off, including Baptist minister Randy Young. "Orlando is a pretty moral town," Young said. "If God was going to hurl a meteor at someone, you'd think he'd start with Las Vegas." (Reuters) ...*Or, more likely, Pat Robertson's house.*

Play Ball: In sports news, the St. Louis Cardinals used their 11th round draft pick to get a pitcher named Vega. Their intent was to draft left-handed pitcher Rene Vega from New York Dominican College. Instead, they accidentally selected Joel Vega, a left-handed pitcher from Ohio Dominican College. "Everybody makes a mistake," Cardinals scouting director Ed Creech said after the error was scored. "It's a little bit embarrassing. No, not a little, a lot embarrassing. I feel sorry for the scout, for the kid we didn't get, for a lot of people." (AP) ...*Not to mention Joel, and the entire state of Ohio.*

Oh, Romeo! The English National Ballet wants its performers to have more spring in their steps in their production of Prokofiev's Romeo and Juliet ballet: it is urging the performers to have sex before the show. "All we are saying is, 'Can you get very amorous off-stage so that you can come and feel your role during the performance'," said spokesman Raymond Gubbay. "This is a very sexually orientated production and without being vulgar, I want it to have more sexual overtones," confirms company artistic director Derek Deane. "They hardly wear anything in the studios and get to touch every part of each other's bodies anyway." (Reuters) ...*"'Tis an ill cook that cannot lick his own fingers." (act 4, scene 2)*

Defensive Play: Japan's state soccer team banned its players from having sex before World Cup games, a Japanese magazine reports. Soccer officials would not comment, except to say, "Even if the report was true, would that cause much of a problem to the players? Every one of them is thinking of nothing but the games." Not so, apparently, the Belgian players. Belgian Eric Deflandre confirms he may have spoken a bit too broadly during an interview. When asked what he was taking to France, he answered "My soccer boots to play soccer and an inflatable doll because a month without a woman would be difficult." After Belgian newspapers published the remark widely, Deflandre insisted the comment was a joke. "[My girlfriend] laughed, even my family laughed. It's just the reporter who didn't laugh." (Reuters, 2) *...Yes, it would seem the reporter is indeed the only one not laughing.*

Liars, Damn Liars, and Politicians: California is considering legislation to prohibit the use of faked photographs in political campaign ads, especially considering how computer techniques makes such fakery easy. The state wants to avoid such situations as an Illinois candidate who published a photograph of himself standing behind the governor at a bill-signing ceremony. In reality, it was his face pasted on a state senator's body. Meanwhile, the Washington Supreme Court struck down a 1984 state law that prohibited candidates from lying in political advertisements. The court said the law chilled political speech, and "assumes the people of this state are too ignorant or disinterested to investigate, learn and determine for themselves the truth or falsity in political debate." (UPI, AP) *...One step forward, two steps back.*

Plaything: Peruzzo Informatica says its new "virtual woman" computer program is merely a "Tamagotchi for adults". The Italian company's "Rachel", which retails for $20, "responds to attention like a real woman" and is "incredibly charming, passionate, capricious." If the program is in a "bad mood", the user can send her flowers to cheer her up. Eventually, Rachel gets "closer and closer to her suitor" and, if he is very successful, she will strip for him. "There's nothing pornographic about it, it's just a game," a Peruzzo spokesman said. (Reuters) *...Just like real life.*

Bull Market: Alan Greenberg, the 70-year-old chairman of the Bear Sterns investment house, has long required employees to give 4 percent of their wages to charity. He is not exempt from his own decree. For his own latest give-away, he is donating $1 million for Viagra prescriptions for people who can't afford the anti-impotence drug. How far will a million bucks go, considering the high cost of the drug? "Depending on demand, I might add to it," Greenberg said. "It can only go up, not down." (AP) *...Either he was talking about the level of his bank account, or he doesn't understand how the drug works.*

Fire in the Hole! Two men fishing in Fox Lake, Ill., threw a lit M-250 firecracker — a "quarter stick of dynamite" — into the water to kill fish. As the fuse burned down, wind blew their aluminum boat to the spot where they had thrown it in. The explosion blew a hole in the bottom of the boat, sinking it. Daniel Wyman, 29, drowned, but his companion swam to safety. (AP) ... *"The worst day fishing beats the best day working." —American idiom.*

<hr>

Grand-Godfather

Mafia Boss Escapes in Wheelchair

AP headline

<hr>

See the World: "There are people who are real offended when you take your pants down in a public street," says Capt. Terrence Riley of the Naval Operational Medicine Institute at Florida's Pensacola Naval Air Station. One of his officers, aerospace physiology instructor Lt. Patrick Callaghan, 28, recently "mooned" a friend while jogging at the military base. Callaghan originally faced charges of indecent exposure and conduct unbecoming an officer, which could have led to his dismissal, but it appears that he will instead only get a letter of reprimand. Callaghan is relieved that he will not be drummed out of the Navy. "Things are looking real good," he said. "I get to continue what I enjoy doing most and that's serve God and my country." (AP) ...*Which was served by baring his butt?*

Sniff: When a police officer found an envelope in Michael Horne's truck, a field test showed it contained methamphetamine and he was arrested. The San Antonio, Texas, officers would not believe Horne when he said the contents were his grandmother's ashes from her cremation. He waited in jail for a month while more sophisticated tests showed they were indeed not speed, but grandma. "Nobody would believe the poor guy no matter how much he screamed and shouted," said Luis Vera, Horne's attorney, who has filed a lawsuit against the city. "You can tell this is ashes when you look at it." And, he was quick to add, "Grandma wasn't a doper." (Reuters) *...Soon to be the title of a Country Western ballad.*

Sniff II: Aurora, Ill., funeral home owner Terry Dieterle is offering a new way to honor the dearly departed. He sells 14-carat gold pendants with a hollow cavity for cremation ashes so survivors can carry a bit of the dead with them at all times. "When your son graduates from high school, he gets a ring," he said. "When you retire, they usually give you a watch. This is just another option." (AP) *...At least someone is trying to put the "fun" back into "funeral".*

Synthetic Son-in-Law: When Rebecca Scott got married on St. Helena, her parents couldn't make the 6,000 mile trip from Middlesbrough, England, to be there. "The only thing to do was stage a virtual wedding," said her mother Maggi. They borrowed two dummies from a local store and dressed them up in wedding suits, invited their friends, and listened to the real ceremony over the phone. "Mum told me that there wasn't a dry eye in the house when the congregation in Middlesbrough heard us say our vows," Rebecca said. Guests then drank champagne toasts and tossed confetti on the dummies. (Reuters) *...Two dummies getting married? Nothing unusual about that.*

Bumper Blabber: Wrentham District Court Judge Daniel Winslow wanted to try out a new punishment on himself before he imposed the sentence on convicted drunk drivers, so he plastered two bright orange stickers on the back of his car: one said "convicted repeat drunk driver", the other urged others to report "erratic driving" to police. "The idea is to remove the mask of anonymity from driving a car and expose one's driving to 1,000 eyes," Winslow said. The Massachusetts judge ruled the experiment a success, saying he got a lot of concerned looks when he drove around town, but no threats or intimidation. He hasn't used the punishment yet, but said he won't hesitate to apply it in an appropriate case. (AP) *...The best part: his teenager stopped asking to borrow the car.*

Bathtub Gin Not a Health Risk: A study by the University of Arizona, Tucson, found that the average home is not very clean. While they found bacteria on kitchen cutting boards, water wrung from dishcloths had the highest germ counts. But one spot was consistently the cleanest. "What we found, and we are still theorizing as to why, is that even before we introduced any disinfectant, the toilet seat was always the cleanest site," said study leader Pat Rusin. (Reuters) ...*Tidy toilet tends to treat tushies tenderly without detergent; knotty contradiction puts testers into tailspin.*

William Tell Wannabe: Larry Slusher and Silas Caldwell, both 47, were drinking buddies. After pounding down a few brews recently, Slusher got an idea: he "put the beer can up on the top of his head and told his buddy to shoot it off," says Bell County (Tenn.) Sheriff Harold Harbin. Unfortunately, "he missed the can and hit [Slusher's] head. I don't think there were any arguments or anything because they were the best of friends." Slusher died two days later from the gunshot, and Caldwell has been charged with murder. (AP) ...*"Never murder a man when he's busy committing suicide." —Woodrow Wilson (1856–1924), U.S. President.*

Frogman: Newsreader Jonathan Hill was reporting the day's news live when a fly flew into his mouth. He "just couldn't spit it out on camera," the Welsh television presenter said later. "It's a tea time show and viewers could have been made ill right across the country" if he spit it out, he said. "I had to be professional with so many people watching. There was only one choice." He swallowed the fly and continued with the broadcast. (Reuters) ...*Hill's new opening line: "And now for the latest buzz."*

Piece Initiative

Israeli Men Say Better Sex
Would Create Social Peace

AFP headline

Extra Headlines . . . .

Research
'Divorce' Magazine Publisher Weds
UPI

• • •

Yeah Yeah, So What?
Group Condemns Latin America Apathy
AP

• • •

You Can Check Out Anytime You Like,
But You Can Never Leave
Can't Afford a Hotel? Try a Convent
AP

Give 'em What They Want
Krapp, Skum Highlight Quest for Global Brand Names
Reuters

• • •

Stop the Presses
Many Cows Not Pregnant
AP

Barbie Cell Phone Sold Separately

Trouble Starts when Bimbo Answers the Phone
Reuters

• • •

Kids Do that Every Evening

Turning Cauliflower to Drama
AP

• • •

At Last, an Honest Public Official

Politician Campaigns for Own Recall
AP

• • •

Gee, Maybe We Should Try It

Insulin Shots May Benefit Diabetics
AP

• • •

Artificial Stupidity

Intel Wants your PC to Watch TV for You
Reuters

Remains Delivered to Widow in
Small Brown Cardboard Box

Founder of CARE Dies

AP

• • •

Vegetarians May Have the Right Idea

Animal Bladders Become Drug Factories

UPI

• • •

Dream Dieter Headline

Rice Cakes, the Silent Killers?

Reuters

• • •

Pass the Belt Sander, Dear

Newlyweds Prefer Home Appliances to Sex: Report

AFP

• • •

Don't Do the Crime if You Can't Do the Time

30 Months for Stealing to Buy Clocks

UPI

• • •

12 to a Box

Judge Drops Cases of Lawyer

UPI

Show Them Who's Boss
Can Powerful Men Deny the Dictates of Their Penis?
Reuters

• • •

Illegal Ones Much More Comfortable
Sex Businesses Chafe Under Legal Chains
UPI

• • •

That's Debatable
Issue of Multiple Debates up for Debate
UPI

• • •

He's Dead, Jim
U.S. Asked to Determine Bones' Fate
AP

• • •

Conclusion After Years of Study
Most Ag Students Want to Be Farmers
AP

You Just Have to Know Where to Look

Tortoise Once Thought Extinct for 150 Years Found in British Zoo

AFP

• • •

So Much for "Family Newspapers"

Here is the Definition of Sex, Mr. President

Reuters

• • •

To be Made into Artificial Plants

Plastics May Grow from Plants in Ten Years

Reuters

• • •

Finally Cleared Out "Something Rotten"

Denmark Returning To Normal

AP

• • •

Zombie

Murdered Woman Found Living in Delhi

AFP

Depends on Your Definition of "Near"

Goldwater's Wife Denies He's Near Death

UPI

Goldwater Dead at 89

UPI the next day

• • •

Achtung!

Germans Stand Proud Without Viagra

AFP

• • •

Candy, Little Girl?

Baptists Try to Lure Strippers Away

AP

• • •

and...

Editor Said Don't Use "Very"

Jet-Powered Ferry is Real Fast

AP

About the Author . . . .

Randy Cassingham has a university degree in journalism, but he has never been a conventional news reporter. His unbounding sense of curiosity has instead led him to explore a number of careers, including commercial photographer, freelance writer, editor, publisher, ambulance paramedic, process engineer, search and rescue sheriff's deputy, after-dinner speaker, and software designer. He is an expert on using the Internet to reach a diverse international audience with entertaining human interest content. Randy lives in Boulder, Colorado.

Photo by Dave Casler

There's Lots More *True*
Where This Came From

This is True® compilations come out every year, pulling together a year's worth of Randy's columns, plus *extra* stories and headlines that didn't fit into his weekly newspaper space. Order the books through your favorite bookstore, or get them directly from us. Just be sure to "Get One for Every Bathroom in the House!"

☐ Send me Volume 1! I need ___ copies of *This is True: Deputy Kills Man With Hammer*

☐ Send me Volume 2! I'd like ___ copies of *This is True: Glow-in-Dark Plants Could Help Farmers*

☐ Send me Volume 3! I must have ___ copies of *This is True: Pit Bulls Love You, Really*

☐ More Volume 4! Send ___ additional copies of this volume, *This is True: Artificial Intelligence Like Real Thing*

Each book is $11, plus $3 total shipping charge for any number of copies ordered. (U.S., Canada, FPO/APO only. Offer may be withdrawn at any time. Write for shipping rates for other countries, or see our web site.)

☐ I'm desperate to get a regular *True* fix every week by e-mail. Sign me up for a full dose every week for just $15 for a full year.

☐ Check or Money Order enclosed

☐ Charge my: ☐ Visa ☐ Mastercard ☐ Discover ☐ AmEx

    Card # _____-_____-_____-_____ (Exp: ___/___)

Name: _____

Address: _____

City _____ State/Prov: _____

Zip/Postal Code: _____ Country: _____

E-mail address: _____

Mail this form with payment to Freelance Communications, PO Box 17326, Boulder CO 80308 USA or see our web site for instant online ordering: http://www.thisistrue.com